"With JESUS"

The Story of Mary Co-redemptrix

"With JESUS"

The Story of Mary Co-redemptrix

Mark Miravalle

Foreword by Edouard Cardinal Gagnon, P.S.S.

QUEENSHIP PUBLISHING

IMPRIMATUR

Ernesto Cardinal Corripio Ahumada,
July 13, 2003

Cover Art: Beato Angelico,
The Coronation of the Virgin,
Uffizi Gallery, Florence.

Library of Congress Number: 2003095632

Published by:
Queenship Publishing
P.O. Box 220
Goleta, CA 93116
(800) 647-9882 (805) 692-0043 FAX: (805) 967-5843
http://www.Queenship.org

Printed in the United States of America

ISBN: 1-57918-241-0

Dedication

To John Paul II

On the occasion of his twenty-fifth anniversary as Vicar of Christ on earth

October 16, 2003

Contents

FOREWORD

The mystery of the Blessed Virgin Mary as "Co-redemptrix of the human race" is a common doctrine of Catholic faith that has been enunciated under this title by modern popes and explained by erudite theologians of the highest respectability within the Church.

The Second Vatican Council was unequivocal about its doctrinal teaching of Marian Coredemption when in paragraph 58 of *Lumen Gentium*, the Council states: "Thus the Blessed Virgin advanced in her pilgrimage of faith, and faithfully persevered in union with her Son unto the cross, where she stood in keeping with the divine command, enduring with her only begotten Son the intensity of his suffering, associated with his sacrifice in her mother's heart, and lovingly consenting to the immolation of this victim which was born of her" (*Lumen Gentium*, 58).

The Holy Father, Pope John Paul II, took this very paragraph on Marian Coredemption from the Council and used it as the principal theme of his 1987 Marian encyclical, *Redemptoris Mater*, which is appropriately named, "Mother of the Redeemer." During his papacy, as is well known, the Holy Father has repeatedly used the title of "Co-redemptrix" and "Co-redemptrix of the human race" in his papal addresses and homilies to the People of God.

Dr. Mark Miravalle, Mariologist from the Franciscan University of Steubenville, has taken great scholarly efforts in bringing to us an impeccably documented history or "story" of the Blessed Virgin as Co-redemptrix, but in a concise format. *"With Jesus"* is an intellectual work that is understandable for any contemporary reader who seeks an honest examination of this Catholic doctrine in Scripture, Tradition, and the teachings of the Church's Magisterium. But *"With Jesus"* is also a work of love from the heart, where the author manifests his own love for his Mother, the Co-redemptrix, and yet without loss of objectivity in this exceptionally documented theological and historical study.

In truth, *how can any faithful Catholic question the appropriateness of the Co-redemptrix title as applied to our Blessed Mother when it has been pronounced by a litany of popes, saints, blesseds, mystics, doctors of the Church, and conciliar theologians throughout the history of the Church, including Pope John Paul II, as documented in this work?*

The title of Co-redemptrix does not threaten the primacy of the Redeemer, any more than St. Paul calling all Christians to be God's "co-workers" (1 Cor. 3:9) threatens the primacy of the Redeemer. We are all called to share in the work of Redemption, and Our Lady, the Co-redemptrix, is our supreme Immaculate example.

As to the eventual papal definition of the doctrine of Co-redemptrix, it is only a matter of time. The doctrine's consistent development throughout Catholic history will eventually bring forth the fruit of the doctrine's perfection on the level of Catholic dogma. This papal proclamation will lead to a greater understanding of this Mariological doctrine, both within the Church and beyond its visible confines. Marian Coredemption is present in the teachings of the great Fathers and Doctors of the Church; and it is present in the powerful prayer of the Holy Rosary, especially in the mysteries of the Annunciation, Presentation, and Crucifixion, which are meditated upon, and happily accepted by the *sensus fidelium*.

That there is controversy over its dogmatic definition is to be expected by any student of the history of Marian Dogmas. Such was the case especially for the dogma of the Mother of God at the Council of Ephesus in 431 and the Immaculate Conception in 1854. Out of the storm of theological debate will come the rainbow of its definition, purified by the storm itself, which will result in its greater clarity and precision in a carefully crafted Marian dogma of faith.

I pray that you enjoy the reading of *"With Jesus,"* that it move your mind and heart for a greater love of the Virgin Mother, who indeed had her soul pierced for you (Lk. 2:35). I also pray that you will pass on this book to the friends or family members who do not yet "behold their Mother" (Jn. 19:27). Most of all, I pray that you will join in prayer, especially the prayer of the Holy Rosary, for the expedient papal proclamation of Our Lady as truly our Co-redemptrix with Jesus.

Edouard Cardinal Gagnon, P.S.S.
President Emeritus, Pontifical Council for the Family
President Emeritus, Pontifical Committee
For International Eucharistic Congresses

AUTHOR'S INTRODUCTION

"With Jesus," from the Annunciation to Calvary: this is the story of Mary Co-redemptrix.

This little work is not primarily for the theologian, but for the reader who, while not necessarily having an extensive theological background, is nonetheless comfortable with citations and notes for the sake of a deeper investigation into this Mariological doctrine and mystery.

I wish to confess to you from the outset, dear reader, my own deep love and gratitude for the Mother whom I hail, as does the Church, as the "Co-redemptrix." But I pray that my personal belief in this Marian mystery will not hamper an objective examination of the question, which must not be based on subjective dispositions, but rather on the objective historic revelation which flows from the Word of God "written," the Sacred Scriptures; the Word of God "oral and handed down," Sacred Tradition; and the guardianship of the Word of God by the Church's Magisterium, all of which is witnessed to and enfleshed in the lives and testimonies of the saints, mystics, popes, and doctors of the Church.

From these sources, I seek to weave a little garland of the story of Mary Co-redemptrix. But just as the Rosary is a brief "compendium of the entire Gospel,"[1] so too this work will be only a brief telling of the whole story, the profundity and sublimity of which not even the world itself could contain the books that would have to be written (cf. Jn. 21:25). For her story is so united to His story that it participates in the very depths and breadth of a God's desire to "buy back" (*redimere*) his people, and in doing so, God willed that this woman be intimately involved in the salvation of the human race.

May the telling of this story, by God's infinite grace, satisfy your mind and bring peace, joy, and gratitude to your heart, for the gift and the mystery of Mary Co-redemptrix.

Notes

[1] Paul VI, Apostolic Exhortation *Marialis Cultus*, 1974, 42.

Chapter I

What Co-redemptrix Does And Does Not Mean

"*When they found you with the Fathers calling her Mother of God, Second Eve, and Mother of all Living, the Mother of Life, the Morning Star, the Mystical New Heaven, the Sceptre of Orthodoxy, the All-undefiled Mother of Holiness, and the like, they would have deemed it a poor compensation for such language, that you protested against her being called a Co-redemptrix . . . .*

—Ven. John Henry Cardinal Newman to Pusey[1]

Ironically, we begin this work by explaining what Mary Co-redemptrix does not mean. This is to avoid initial misconceptions that can prejudice the term, quite apart from how the Church, that is, popes, saints, doctors, mystics and martyrs, has in fact used it. It is one thing to espouse that "I do not accept the Church calling the Mother of Jesus the 'Co-redemptrix,'" to reject the title due to a misconception of what the Church herself denotes by it. It is a different and intellectually unjust matter to maintain that the Church means something other than what she says she means when she calls the Mother of Jesus the "Co-redemptrix."

What does "Co-redemptrix" *not* mean in the

teachings of the Catholic Church? It does not mean that Mary is a goddess, that she is the fourth person of the Trinity, that she in any way possesses a divine nature, that she is in any fashion not a creature completely dependent upon her Creator like all other creatures. In quoting one of the greatest Marian saints of Church history, St. Louis Marie Grignion de Montfort, I join with him and the entire Church in asserting the Christian truth of Mary's unquestionable creaturehood and total dependence on the Divine Lord of all, and that God has no absolute need for the participation of the Mother of Jesus for the accomplishment of his divine will:

> I avow, with all the Church, that Mary, being a mere creature who has come from the hands of the Most High, is in comparison with His Infinite Majesty less than an atom; or rather, she is nothing at all, because only He is "He who is" (Exod. 3:14); consequently that grand Lord, always independent and sufficient to Himself, never had, and has not now, any absolute need of the holy Virgin for the accomplishment of His will and for the manifestation of His glory. He has but to will in order to do everything.[2]

The truth embodied by the Church's doctrine concerning the Virgin Mary applies entirely to the subject of Redemption. The Church maintains that Mary's participation in the Redemption accomplished by Jesus Christ, truly God and truly man, was by no means absolutely necessary. Moreover, Mary herself, as a creature and a daughter of Adam and Eve within the human family was in need of being preserved from the effects of original sin, and thereby was wholly dependent upon her Son-Redeemer for her own exalted form of Redemption.

Any concept of Mary Co-redemptrix, therefore, that suggests the Mother of Jesus is a fourth Trinitarian person or some type of goddess must be immediately and entirely rejected as grave heresy against Christian revelation. Such blatant error clouds the real theological issues surrounding the doctrine of Co-redemptrix, such as: the nature and limits of human participation in a divine work; the mysterious balance between Divine Providence and human freedom in salvation; the role of human cooperation in the individual distribution of the graces of Redemption; the divine desire to have a woman directly partake in the restoration of grace and its effects on personal human dignity, and several other relevant themes.

What then does the Church mean when she calls the Blessed Virgin Mary the "Co-redemptrix?" Let us first look at the etymological meaning of the title itself.

The prefix, "co-" derives from the Latin term "*cum*," which means "with" (and not "equal to"). Although some modern languages, such as English, sometimes use the prefix "co" with connotations of equality, the true Latin meaning remains "with." And in English, for example, the prefix "co" is at other times properly used to signify "with" in a context of subordination or dependence, in cases such as "pilot and co-pilot"; "star and co-star"; "Creator and co-creator" in the theology of the body and nuptial love, and so forth.

In the revealed word of God, St. Paul identifies the early Christians as "co-workers with God" (1 Cor. 3:9) in a meaning and context of "co" which cannot possibly denote equality. So, too, are we "co-heirs" with Christ (Rom. 8:17), without meaning that we are equally heirs to heaven as the only-begotten Son of God is heir to Heaven.

The Latin verb, "*redimere*" (or re[d]-emere), signifies literally " to buy back." The Latin suffix, "-trix" is feminine, denoting "one who does something." The etymological meaning of Co-redemptrix therefore refers to the "*woman with the Redeemer,*" or more literally: "the woman who buys back with."

In summation, then, the title "Mary Co-redemptrix" as used by the Church denotes the unique and active participation by Mary, the Mother of Jesus, in the work of Redemption as accomplished by Jesus Christ, the divine and human Redeemer. The title of Co-redemptrix never places Mary on a level of equality with Jesus Christ, the divine Lord of all, in the accomplishment of human salvation. It would wound the Heart of Mary more than any other heart, hers an immaculate and transparent Heart created to reflect perfectly the glories of her Son,[3] if she were to be mistakenly perceived as an equal or parallel redeemer with her own divine Son.

The Co-redemptrix title, rather, identifies Mary's singular and unparalleled sharing with her Son in the restoration of grace for the human family. The Mother of the Redeemer participates in a wholly secondary and subordinate way in the buying back of humanity with and under her Divine Son. For *Jesus Christ alone* in his divinity, the Sovereign Alpha and Omega, could satisfy the just compensation for the sins of mankind necessary in reconciling humanity with God, the Father of all mankind.

Jesus Christ, truly God and truly man, is the Redeemer of the universe. Mary, the Church teaches, is the woman completely "with the Redeemer" who like no other creature, angel or saint, shared in his saving work. She gave Jesus her own flesh and blood; she suffered with Jesus in all his earthly suffering; she walked with Jesus the steps to Calvary; she offered with Jesus at Golgotha in obedience to the Father; she died with Jesus in her Heart. What does the Church mean when she calls Mary the Co-redemptrix? In a phrase: Mary is *"With Jesus," from the Annunciation to Calvary.*

This is why St. Louis de Montfort concludes his statement regarding the Virgin Mother of God by positively stating that her role in salvation, though not in the order of absolute necessity, is in the order of God's perfect and manifest will:

> Nevertheless, I say that, things being as they are now — that is, God having willed to

> commence and complete His greatest works by the most holy Virgin ever since He created Her — we may well think He will not change His conduct in the eternal ages; for He is God, and He changes not, either in His sentiments or in His conduct.[4]

The question for the disciple of Christ is not, "what was absolutely necessary, so that I may accept it?" but rather, "what was God's manifest will, that I may believe it?" It was God's manifest will that a woman and a mother be directly and intensely involved "with the Redeemer," in the buying back of the human family from Satan and the effects of sin. Because of this role, which exceeds all other human and creaturely roles, the Mother of Jesus uniquely lays claim to the title of Co-redemptrix, "with Jesus" in the atoning work of human Redemption. It is a title given to her by the Church, and it is rightfully hers more than any other creature, beyond all other Christians who are called to be "co-redeemers."[5] For the Immaculate Mother alone is spiritually crucified at Calvary in an experience of maternal suffering that is almost beyond human imagination.[6]

It is Mary, not the Church, who first gives birth to the Redeemer. It is the fruit of Mary's suffering with and under the Redeemer that leads to the mystical birth of the Church at Calvary (Jn. 19:25-27). It is precisely this mystical birth by the New Eve, the new "Mother of the Living,"[7] which makes it possible for us to become co-redeemers within the mysterious and salvific distribution of graces which flow from Calvary.

The historical person of Mary, Virgin of Nazareth, through her lifetime cooperation "with Jesus" in the work of Redemption, becomes, in the words of John Paul II, the "Co-redemptrix of humanity."[8]

Perhaps, too, the words of one contemporary Anglican Oxford scholar, who here travels in the footprints of another Oxford scholar, Venerable Cardinal Newman, will compel us toward a new open-mindedness to the Co-redemptrix title and its further explanation within Christian Revelation:

> The matter cannot be settled by pointing to the dangers of exaggeration and abuse, or by appealing to isolated texts of scripture such as 1 Timothy 2:5, or by the changing fashions in theology and spirituality, or by the desire not to say anything that might offend one's partners in ecumenical dialogue. Unthinking enthusiasts may have elevated Mary to a position of virtual equality with Christ, but this aberration is not a *necessary* consequence of recognizing that there may be a truth striving for expression in words like *Mediatrix* and *Coredemptrix*. All responsible theologians would agree that Mary's co-redemptive role is subordinate and auxiliary to the central role of Christ. But if she does have such a role, the more clearly we understand it, the better. It is a matter for

theological investigation. And, like other doctrines concerning Mary, it is not only saying something about her, but something more general concerning the Church as a whole or even humanity as a whole.[9]

Notes

[1] Ven. John Cardinal Newman, *Certain Difficulties Felt by Anglicans in Catholic Teaching Considered*, vol. 2, *In a Letter Addressed to the Rev. E. B. Pusey, D.D., On Occasion of His Eirenicon of 1864*, Longman's, Green and Co., 1891, vol. 2, p. 78.

[2] St. Louis Marie Grignion de Montfort, *True Devotion to Mary*, ch. 1, n. 14.

[3] For example, Lk. 1:46: "my soul magnifies the Lord" and Jn. 2:5: "do whatever he tells you."

[4] De Montfort, *True Devotion to Mary*, ch. 1, n. 15.

[5] Cf. John Paul II, Address to the sick at the Hospital of the Brothers of St. John of God, April 5, 1981, *L'Osservatore Romano*, English edition, April 13, 1981, p. 6; General Audience, Jan. 13, 1982, *Inseg.* V/1, 1982, 91; Address to candidates for the Priesthood, Montevideo, May 8, 1988, *L'Osservatore Romano*, English edition, May 30, 1988, p. 4; cf. Pius XI, Papal Allocution at Vicenza, Nov. 30, 1933.

[6] John Paul II, Apostolic Letter *Salvifici Doloris*, Feb. 11, 1984, 25; *AAS* 76, 1984, p. 214.

[7] Cf. Gen. 3:20.

[8] Cf. Pius XI, Papal Allocution at Vicenza; John Paul II, General Audience, Sept. 8, 1982; *Inseg.* V/3, 1982, 404.

[9] J. Macquarrie, "Mary Co-redemptrix and Disputes Over Justification and Grace: An Anglican View," *Mary Co-redemptrix: Doctrinal Issues Today*, Queenship, 2002, p. 140.

Chapter II

Co-redemptrix Foretold

It is one thing to define a term; it is quite another to believe it. That the Church defines the meaning of Co-redemptrix as Mary's entirely unique sharing in the work of Redemption with Jesus is clear. But on what basis does she believe it to be true?

God's perfect providence, dictated not by absolute necessity, but by divine disposition, the Heart of God expressed to the heart of man, is revealed in a primary way through Sacred Scripture.

The Mother of Jesus is rightly understood not as a woman in Scripture, but as *The Woman of Scripture*. She is, as we shall see, the "woman" of Genesis (Gen. 3:15), the "woman" of Cana (Jn. 2:4), the "woman" of Calvary (Jn. 19:25), the "woman" of Revelation (Rev. 12:1), and the "woman" of Galatians (Gal. 4:4).

But here we must ponder the revelation of the Woman of Scripture specific to her role "with Jesus" in the work of Redemption. We commence with the ancient Covenant between God and man and its written Testament.

The Great Prophecy - Genesis 3:15[1]
"I will put enmity between you and the woman"

We begin at the beginning, in the Book of Genesis with the *protoevangelium* ("first gospel"). For the merciful love of the Father permits fallen humanity to be in despair without a redeemer for only a few verses.

After the human "sin of sins" takes place, God is quick to reveal his redemptive plan to reverse or "recapitulate," as the early Fathers would say, the sin of Adam and Eve. The Creator in his omniscience makes known a plan to bring about the serpent's complete defeat by using the same basic means, though in reverse, by which Satan effected the loss of grace for the human family. In doing so, God the Father of all mankind further reveals his omnipotent sovereignty over Satan.

God reveals his redemptive plan of a future woman and her future "seed" of victory: "I will put enmity between you and the woman, and between your seed and her seed; he (she) shall crush your head, and you shall lie in wait for his (her) heel (Gen. 3:15)."

In this greatest of Old Testament prophecies, we see a struggle between a woman and her offspring (or "seed") against Satan and his seed of evil and sin. With the revelation of the battle is the revelation of the eventual victory of the woman and her seed in the crushing of Satan's head.

The "seed" who is ultimately victorious over Satan and his seed can refer only to Jesus Christ. No one else may lay claim to the redemptive victory of the crucified and resurrected Redeemer. The "woman" of the seed of victory must then also refer to Mary in the most essential and ultimate sense, who is alone the true and natural mother of Jesus Christ. Eve does not give physical birth to the Redeemer, nor does Israel, nor does the Church. Only Mary the "New Eve" does.

This Genesis passage is quintessentially prophetic, foretelling a definitive victory over Satan to take place *in the future* ("I will put"). So, too, must the two persons of the victory be in the future, so that through a woman yet to be born and her victorious seed, the loss of the first woman would be vindicated.

God places "enmity" between the woman and the serpent and their respective "seeds." "Enmity" in scripture refers to a complete and radical opposition,[2] and it is precisely this enmity which separates the woman and her seed (Mother and Son) from Satan and his seed. *It is within this divinely-established enmity that the nature and role of Mary Co-redemptrix is first foretold.*

The woman shares with her seed in the struggle against the serpent and his seed. In the full light of salvation history, we understand that this passage foreshadows Mary, Mother of the Redeemer, who intimately shares in the identical struggle against Satan and evil as does Jesus the Redeemer. The Woman "with Jesus" participates in the great battle for buying back humanity, which is revealed by the Heavenly Father immediately after the first woman participates in the loss of humanity "with Adam." Eve becomes the "co-peccatrix" ("with the sinner"); Mary is prophesied as the "Co-redemptrix" ("with the redeemer").[3]

The "enmity" between the woman and the serpent also foretells the "Immaculate One," who is both free from sin and full of grace. Only a person in total and complete opposition to the Evil One could be entirely immaculate or "stainless" (*macula*, "stain"). In its positive meaning, this Woman will be "full of grace" (Lk. 1:28), for she positively bears the full fruits of Redemption applied to her in an exalted way, in a preservative way, through which she will never be touched by Satan and his sinful seed.[4]

The Heavenly Father's "Immaculate One," His Virgin Daughter full of grace, will represent humanity in the battle "with Jesus" for souls. She will be God's greatest masterpiece, his greatest creature, fighting against his most heinous creature in this cosmic struggle. Only one free from sin could be an appropriate partner with the Redeemer in the work of Redemption. A sin-stained partner would be acting as a type of double agent, working with the Redeemer and with Satan at the same time. Mary will be the Co-redemptrix entirely and exclusively "with Jesus," because she is first the Immaculate Conception.[5] Her freedom from sin from the moment of conception will be God's gift to mankind, and her "fiat," freely given, will represent mankind's response. The necessity of this freedom, this total giving of self, is essential, for God respects absolutely the free cooperation of his creatures in the work of human salvation.

"She will crush your head." The revelation of the Co-redemptrix in Genesis 3:15 does not depend upon the debated pronoun translation ("he" or "she") of this second line of the prophecy. It is revealed first in the Eternal Father's foretelling of the future battle in which Mary, woman of the "seed," mother of the redeemer, will intrinsically participate with her Son against those with whom they have enmity, Satan and his seed.

It is nonetheless noteworthy that in the revealed text, it is the woman who must struggle directly against the serpent, while the seed of the woman is in parallel struggle against the seed of the serpent. If we are to properly respect the parallelism in the text, it is appropriate to conclude from the first "enmity" announced between the woman and the serpent, that the subsequent pronouns then logically refer to the first protagonist, the woman, and the first antagonist, the serpent. The pronoun "she" thereby refers to the woman-protagonist crushing the "head" of the serpent-antagonist.[6]

The traditional Vulgate which conveys the Genesis passage with the female pronoun, "*ipsa*" or "she" has been used by numerous popes in papal documents in referring to Mary. For example, Bl. Pius IX in the papal bull defining the Immaculate Conception, *Ineffabilis Deus* (Dec. 8, 1854), refers to the woman of Genesis 3:15 as Mary, who will crush the head of Satan "with her virginal foot" and clearly identifies the Mother's sharing in the Son's redemptive victory. This is but one of several examples from the papal magisterium that identify without question the woman of

Genesis 3:15 as Mary:

> The Fathers and ecclesiastical writers, enlightened by instruction from on high, taught that the divine prophecy: "I will put enmity between you and the woman, between your seed and her seed," clearly and plainly foretold how there was to be a merciful Redeemer for mankind, namely, the only-begotten Son of God, Jesus Christ. They also taught how the prophecy pointed to His Blessed Mother, the Virgin Mary, and how it clearly expressed at the same time their common enmity toward the devil. Just as Christ, the Mediator between God and men, by taking our nature, cancelled the decree of condemnation against us, triumphantly nailing it to the cross, so too the most holy Virgin, intimately and indissolubly united to Christ, became with Him the everlasting enemy of the venomous serpent, and thus shared with Her Son His victory over the serpent, crushing as she did the serpent's head with her virginal foot.[7]

It is telling that Our Lady herself does not appear to be hindered by a pronoun translation debate when in the Church-approved Miraculous Medal apparitions of

Our Lady of Grace at Rue de Bac (Nov. 27, 1830), the vision and subsequent medal depict the Mediatrix of all graces as literally stepping on the head of the serpent with her foot.[8]

Mary Co-redemptrix is the Woman of Genesis 3:15. But she is also the Woman and the Virgin Mother of Isaiah, who in another great Old Testament prophecy is foretold in bringing forth the great sign of salvation predicted to Ahaz: "Behold a virgin shall conceive and bear a son, and shall call his name, Immanuel" (Is. 7:14). She is further the Woman of Micah, who "in travail" brings forth the future ruler who will save Israel: "But you, O Bethlehem Ephrathah, who are little to be among the clans of Judah, from you shall come forth one who is to be ruler in Israel, whose origin is from old, from ancient days. Therefore he shall give them up until the time when she who is in travail has brought forth, then the rest of his brethren shall return to the people of Israel" (Mic. 5:2-3). The prophecy of the travail of the woman refers not to birth pains due to sin, inapplicable to the Immaculata conceived without original sin and its effects, but rather to the co-suffering that awaits the Mother of the Redeemer in giving spiritual birth to the many at the greatest of prices.

Old Testament Types and Symbols of the Co-redemptrix

And what of the many great women of the Old Testament, who in their very persons foretell of the Co-redemptrix to come?

Sarah, wife of Abraham, through a miraculous birth, gives birth to Isaac and becomes the "Mother of nations" (Gen. 17:15-17). Mary, through a miraculous birth, gives birth to the Redeemer and becomes the Mother of all peoples (cf. Lk. 1:38, Jn. 19:25-27).

Rebecca dresses Jacob in the clothing of Esau to obtain the inheritance of the first born from his father, Isaac (cf. Gen. 25:1-40). Mary dresses Jesus in the clothing of humanity to obtain for the rest of the human family the inheritance of the Heavenly Father.

Rachel gives birth to Joseph, the future savior for the tribe of Jacob, who is sold for twenty pieces of silver by his own brethren (cf. Gen. 37:28). Mary gives birth to Jesus, the future savior of all people, who is sold for thirty pieces of silver (cf. Mt. 26:15).

The prophetess Deborah is Barak's active partner in the victory over Sisera (which leads to the crushing of Sisera's head by Jael), for which Deborah later proclaims a hymn of exultation (cf. Judg. 4:5). Mary, Queen of Prophets is the active partner with Christ in the victory over sin and the crushing of Satan's head, for which she proclaims the greatness of the Lord (cf. Lk. 1:46).

The valiant Judith battles against the enemy Holofernes, and triumphs over him with the cutting off of his head (cf. Jud. 8-16). The valiant Mary battles against Satan, and triumphs over him with the crushing of his head (cf. Gen. 3:15, Jn. 19:27).

Queen Esther finds favor with King Ahasuerus in risking her life to save her people from a decree of death.

Mary Co-redemptrix finds favor with Christ the King in offering her life for the mission of Redemption in the saving of all people "with Jesus" from the decree of eternal death (Lk. 1:38).

A phenomenal Old Testament type of Mary Co-redemptrix is found in the noble "Mother of Macabees" (cf. 2 Mac. 7). Under a persecution from the secular king, Antiochus, six sons, one after the other, are torturously murdered in the presence of their mother because of their fidelity to the fasting practices of the Covenant. Antiochus himself calls upon the mother to intervene with her seventh son to save himself by accepting the offers of wealth and power from the king, if the son will only turn away from the fasting disciplines of the Covenant. The mother instead takes the opportunity to appeal to her son with words of encouragement and exhortation, instructing him to, "accept death, so that in God's mercy I may get you back again with your brothers" (2 Mac. 7:29).

How eloquently the Mother of Maccabees foreshadows the story of Mary Co-redemptrix! The seven swords of sorrow that will pierce the Mother's heart are predicted in the sufferings of the seven sons of Maccabees. The courageous glance, amidst the necessary tears, from the face of the Mother directed to the face of the crucified Son at Calvary convey in a message beyond words the imperative to persevere in the redemptive plan of the New and everlasting Covenant. The temptations of wealth, power, fame, or even the "futility" of the upcoming crucifixion whispered to the Son by the Prince of this world, are countered by the witness of humility, poverty, and obedience manifested by the faithful Virgin Mother, who herself wholly Immaculate, is the greatest and most worthy fruit of the Redemption wrought by her Son.

The scriptural account of the Mother of Macabees and her seven sons ends with the words: "Last of all, the mother died, after her sons" (2 Mac. 7:41). So too, the popes tell us, does the Mother Co-redemptrix experience at Calvary a true "dying with Him in her heart, pierced by the sword of sorrow,"[9] where the Mother of the Redeemer is "crucified spiritually with her crucified son."[10]

The Mother Co-redemptrix is moreover foretold in the greatest of all Marian symbols of the Old Testament, the "Ark of the Covenant." The Ark is the place of "God's presence," bearing fragments of the tablet of the Ten Commandments, the staff of Aaron, and the mysterious manna from heaven, which together represent the law, the priesthood, and the sustaining food of the Covenant. As such the Ark is the concrete sign of the saving covenant between Yahweh and the people of Israel (cf. Deut 31:25; Ex. 16:4-36; Num. 17:1-13).

Likewise, the Mother of the Redeemer bears within herself Christ the New Law, Christ the High Priest, and Christ the Eucharist, which makes her the supreme Ark of the New Covenant. She is the divinely created and crafted bearer of the new and eternal covenant between divinity and humanity, the free and active Ark made of incorruptible wood, who both bears and suffers with the High Priest of the Everlasting Covenant.

Every groaning of the Old Testament yearns forward to the Incarnation and to the fulfilled mission of Christ the Redeemer. And every longing for the redeeming Son is also, according to the saving plan of the Eternal Father, a longing for the co-redeeming Mother. For, as Blessed Pope Pius IX instructs in the dogmatic proclamation of the Immaculate Conception, both the Redeemer and the Co-redemptrix were indissolubly willed by the Father of all mankind to partake in the mission of human Redemption in "one and the same decree."[11]

Notes

---

[1] For extended commentaries, cf. T. Gallus, S.J., *Interpretatio mariologica Protoevangelii*, vol. 1, *Tempore post-patristico ad Concilium Tridentinum*, Rome, 1949; vol. 2, *A Concilio Tridentino usque ad annum 1660*, Rome, 1953; vol. 3 *Ab anno 1661 usque ad definitionem dogmaticum Immaculatae Conceptionis (1854)*, Rome, 1954; cf. D. Unger, O.F.M.Cap., "Patristic Interpretation of the Protoevangelium," *Marian Studies*, vol. 12, 1961, pp. 111-164; cf. A. Bea, S.J., "Il Protoevangelio [Gen. 3:15] nella tradizione esegetica," *L'Osservatore Romano*, Oct. 30, 1954, p. 1; "Maria SS. Nel Protovangelo (Gen. 3:15)," *Marianum*, vol. 15, 1953, pp. 1-21; cf. S. Manelli, F.F.I., *All Generations Shall Call Me Blessed*, Academy of the Immaculate, 1995; "Mary Co-redemptrix in Sacred Scripture," *Mary Coredemptrix, Mediatrix, Advocate Theological Foundations II*, Queenship, 1996, pp. 71-80.

[2] For other examples of "enmity" in Scripture, cf. Num. 35:21-22, Deut. 4:42, Deut. 19:4, 6.

[3] Cf. Alfons Maria Cardinal Stickler, *Maria: Mitterloserin*, Salzburg, Dec. 9, 1990, *Informationsblatt der Priesterbruderschaft St. Petrus*, n. 12, Wigratzbad, Jahrgang, 1991.

[4] Bl. Pius IX, Apostolic Constitution *Ineffabilis Deus*, 1854.

[5] Karol Cardinal Wojtyla, Homily on the Feast of the Immaculate Conception, December 8, 1973; cf. John Paul II, General Audience, Dec. 7, 1983, *L'Osservatore Romano*, English edition, December 12, 1983, p. 2; General Audience, Jan. 24, 1996, *L'Osservatore Romano*, English edition, January 31, 1996, p. 11; cf. also H. M. Manteau-Bonamy, O.P., *Immaculate Conception and the Holy Spirit: The Marian Teachings of St. Maximilian Kolbe*, trans. by R. Arnandez, F.S.C., Franciscan Marytown Press, 1977, chs. 2, 7.

[6] For an extended discussion of the parallelism of the Genesis 3:15 text, and a defense of the ipsa ("she") pronoun from historical and medieval commentaries, particularly Cornelius à Lapide, cf. Bro. Thomas Sennott, M.I.C.M., "Mary Co-redemptrix," *Mary at the*

Foot of the Cross II: Acts of the International Symposium on Marian Coredemption, Academy of the Immaculate, 2002, pp. 49-63. The author offers the following initial explanation in support of ipsa and quotes Cornelius à Lapide in support:

"In Hebrew *hu* is 'he,' and *he* 'she,' . . . There is no 'it' in Hebrew, both *hu* and *he* can be translated 'it' depending on the context.

In Greek 'he' is *autos*, 'she' *aute*, and 'it' *auto*.

In Latin 'he' is *ipse*, 'she' *ipsa*, and 'it' *ipsum* . . .

Cornelius à Lapide in his great *Commentaria in Scripturam Sacram* says that the underlying mystery is even reflected in the Hebrew grammar. 'Also *hu* is often used instead of *he* especially when there is some emphasis on action and something manly is predicated of the woman, as is the case here with the crushing *of* the serpent's head . . . It makes no difference that the verb is masculine *yasuph*, that is "(he) shall crush," for it often happens in Hebrew that the masculine is used instead of the feminine and vice versa, especially when there is an underlying reason or mystery, as I have just said' (C. à Lapide, *Commentaria in Scripturam Sacram*, Larousse, Paris, 1848, p. 105). The 'underlying mystery' is, of course, that Our Lady crushes the head of the serpent by the power of Our Lord."

[7] Bl. Pius IX, *Ineffabilis Deus*; For other papal magisterial or conciliar references citing Mary's unique role in Redemption as revealed in the Genesis 3:15 passage, cf. Leo XIII, Encyclical *Augustissimae Virginis*, 1897; *ASS* 30, p. 129; St. Pius X, Encyclical *Ad Diem Illum*, Feb. 2, 1904; *ASS* 36, p. 462; Pius XI, Encyclical *Divini Redemptoris*, 1937; *AAS* 29, p. 96; Pius XII, Apostolic Constitution *Munificentissimus Deus*, 1937; *AAS* 42, p. 768; Encyclical *Fulgens Corona*, 1953; *AAS* 45, p. 579; Second Vatican Council, *Lumen Gentium*, 55; Paul VI, Apostolic Letter *Signum Magnum*, May 13, 1967; John Paul II, Encyclical *Redemptoris Mater*, March 25, 1987.

[8] See the descriptions of the apparitions found in R. Laurentin, *Catherine Labouré et la Médaille Miraculeuse*, Paris, 1976.

[9] Leo XIII, Encyclical *Jucunda Semper*, Sept. 8, 1894; *ASS* 27, 1894-1895, p. 178.

[10] John Paul II, in an Address at the Marian shrine in Guayaquil, Ecuador on January 31, 1985, *L'Osservatore Romano*, English edition, March 11, 1985, p. 7.

[11] Bl. Pius IX, *Ineffabilis Deus*.

Chapter III

Co-redemptrix Begun

"*Incarnatio redemptiva redemptio inchoativa*" ("the redemptive Incarnation is the Redemption begun"). This patristic concept of the miracle of miracles in which the Second person of the Most Holy Trinity deigned to become flesh for us correctly conveys that the Incarnation of Jesus Christ is truly the "Redemption begun." And yet, it was the Father's perfect plan that such redemptive Incarnation take place only through the consent of a human, a woman, a virgin.

"Yes" to the Annunciation: Lk. 1: 26-38
"Let it be done to me according to your word"

Perhaps St. Bernard describes it best when he states that the whole world waited to hear the response of the Virgin, upon whom salvation was dependent: "The angel awaits an answer; . . . We too are waiting O Lady, for your word of compassion; the sentence of condemnation weighs heavily upon us . . . We shall be set free at once if you consent . . . This is what the whole earth waits for . . . ." St. Luke records the commencement of Redemption:

> In the sixth month the angel Gabriel was sent from God to a city of Galilee named Nazareth, to a virgin betrothed to a man whose name was Joseph, of the house of David; and the virgin's name was Mary. And he came to her and said, "Hail, full of grace, the Lord is with you!" But she was greatly troubled at the saying, and considered in her mind what sort of greeting this might be. And the angel said to her, "Do not be afraid, Mary, for you have found favor with God. And behold, you will conceive in your womb and bear a son, and you shall call his name Jesus.
>
> He will be great and will be called
> the Son of the Most High;
> and the Lord God will give to him
> the throne of his father David,
> and he will reign over the house of Jacob
> for ever;
> and of his kingdom there will be no end."
>
> And Mary said to the angel, "How can this be since I know not man?"
>
> And the angel said to her,
> "The Holy Spirit will come upon you, and
> the power of the Most High
> will overshadow you;

therefore the child to be born will be called
holy, the Son of God.
And behold, your kinswoman Elizabeth in her old age has also conceived a son; and this is the sixth month with her who was called barren. For nothing is impossible with God." And Mary said, "Behold, I am the handmaid of the Lord; let it be done to me according to your word." And the angel departed from her.

"Be it done unto me according to your word." With these words, words of a free and immaculate virgin, the Word became flesh and dwelt among us. "The Eternal Father entrusted himself to the Virgin of Nazareth," and the Virgin gave her "yes" to the Father's plan to redeem the world through the incarnate Son.

For those tempted to dismiss the "fiat of history" as bereft of any real active participation on the part of the Virgin (as if her consent was only a type of passive recognition or simple submission), Mary's "fiat" in the Greek is expressed in the optative mood (*ghenòito moi . . .*), a mood which expresses her active and joyful desire, not merely a passive acceptance, to participate in the divine plan.

Redemption Begun — Co-redemption Begun

As the Incarnation is the *Redemption begun*, so too is Mary's fiat the *Co-redemption begun*. In the words of

Blessed Teresa of Calcutta, "Of course, Mary is the Co-redemptrix. She gave Jesus his body, and the body of Jesus is what saved us." The Letter to the Hebrews tells us that we have been "sanctified by the offering of the body of Jesus Christ, once for all" (Heb. 10:10). But Jesus receives the precious instrument of Redemption, his sacred body, through Mary. In virtue of the intimate and sublime salvific gift, body to Body, heart to Heart, Mother to Son, the Immaculate Virgin begins her role as Co-redemptrix in the donation of human nature — from the Co-redemptrix to the Redeemer.

But within the gift of body from Mary to Jesus, is the gift of heart bespoken in that gift of body. It is the gift of free will, of soul and spirit, unconditionally offered back to the Eternal Father, in the "yes" of the Immaculate One to His redemptive plan, regardless of the price.

With this "let it be done to me," the humble Virgin of Nazareth becomes "cause of salvation for herself and the whole human race" as St. Irenaeus teaches; the "price of the redemption of captives" as St. Ephraem proclaims; she "conceived redemption for all" as St. Ambrose explains; and is rightly greeted, "Hail, redemption of the tears of Eve" by the eastern Akathist Hymn. St. Augustine tells us that the faithful Virgin first bore Christ in her heart and then in her flesh; and St. Thomas Aquinas explains that the Blessed Virgin's free consent to receive the Word represented in a true sense the consent of the entire human race to receive the Eternal Son as the Redeemer.

The Immaculate One's "yes," soft-spoken to the

Archangel Gabriel, is amplified and resounds throughout creation and time. It is humanity's yes by humanity's best, for she speaks not only for herself but in the name of mankind, when she gives her assent to the Father's design for a Redeemer. The Triune God so respects human free will, typically fragile and fickle, that he awaits human consent for a mission upon which literally every human soul's eternal destiny depends. Yet, above all human creatures, the sinless Mary is most free to choose, most able to offer herself to the Father for the accomplishment of his will. And when her consent is given, he generously responds.

Theologians have long examined the precise nature of Mary's fiat in relation to her role in Redemption, and have sought to categorize it. Some have argued that her fiat is only a "remote," "indirect" or "mediate" participation in the plan of Redemption, too distant from Calvary to be considered an intimate sharing in the accomplishment of Redemption. But in this we must remember the wisdom of the early Church Fathers, who teach that the Incarnation *is the Redemption anticipated and begun.*

If we examine the question from the perspective of God the Father of all mankind, further light is to be found: The Father sends an angelic invitation to his Immaculate Virgin Daughter, requesting of her a free assent to become the greatest human cooperator in the plan of Redemption by becoming the Mother of the Redeemer, including everything that is *mysteriously part of that redemptive plan and role.*

There are not two invitations. There is not one for bearing the Redeemer and another for suffering *with* the Redeemer — not one invitation sent to Nazareth and another sent to Calvary. Mary is invited by the Almighty to a vocation of the greatest conceivable union with the Redeemer and with His prophesied mission. The redemptive mission begins with the Immaculate One giving the Logos flesh, but it certainly does not end there. The Virgin knows that hers is a historical and lifetime vocation, that she is to become the Mother of the "Suffering Servant" of Isaiah — the messianic mission, of which the Virgin, educated in the Temple, is well knowledgeable. Her vocation is a celestial call for an extraordinary lifelong suffering. It is an invitation to a vocation of being "with Jesus," beginning at the Annunciation and continuing in heart wherever the Redeemer goes and whatever the Redeemer does. Always she will be his constant companion in suffering. At Calvary, the Virgin Daughter of the Father understands clearly that her consent to co-suffer in the great immolation of her Victim-Son was given thirty-three years earlier at Nazareth.

Is this not the same with the "yes" that one utters to the various Christian vocations? The priest, the religious, the married person say "yes" on the day of ordination, profession, or marriage, accepting a lifetime of service and love in that vocation, without the knowledge of everything the vocation will entail in the future. Is the priest on the day of ordination given divine illumination regarding each and every specific joy and sorrow that awaits him in the life of priesthood? Rather his "yes" on the day of ordination is a "yes" to the entire plan of the Eternal Father for his vocation. The Father need not issue a second invitation before the most climactic aspects of his priestly sacrifice numerous years later, for the first "yes" of the priest is a lifetime "yes" to the entire life vocation.

The vocational "yes" of the Virgin of Nazareth is a lifetime "yes" to suffering "with Jesus," from the Annunciation to Calvary and beyond. Seen in this light, Mary's fiat not only begins her providential vocation as Co-redemptrix with Jesus, but it also begins an intimately willed and consented participation in the Father's redemptive plan with the Son *in its entirety*, in whatever manner the mission of Redemption with Jesus is to unfold historically in act and circumstance.

Mary, with the fullest consent of her heart and spirit, cooperates "with Jesus" in the redemptive plan of the Father from that Annunciation "fiat." There is never a time when she is not intimately, morally and directly cooperating with Jesus in the developing redemptive plan of the Father, which only reaches full maturity and mystical birth at Calvary. "*Principium huius maternitatis est munus Corredemptricis*" ("the beginning of this maternity is the office of Co-redemptrix"). For this reason, it is best to describe the singular role of Mary in the plan of Redemption initiated at the Annunciation as the "*Co-redemptrix begun*," and her climactic participation "with Jesus" at Calvary as the "*Co-redemptrix fulfilled.*"

Joseph's Ordeal and Mary's Heart

Soon after the fiat, an intensity of suffering begins for her. The Immaculate One becomes physically recognizable as pregnant. She is the Tabernacle of the Redeemer, but this is not yet known or understood by others. The Virgin's suffering is multiplied by the suffering of one so close, so dear, so just, that it increases the sacrificial offering of her young heart. It is the ordeal of Joseph.

"When his mother Mary had been betrothed to Joseph, before they came together she was found to be with child of the Holy Spirit; and her husband Joseph, being a just man and unwilling to put her to shame, resolved to send her away quietly" (Mt. 1:18-19). After the Virgin's return from Ain-Karim, during which for three months the Icon of Charity exercised her virtues at the service of Elizabeth, Joseph witnessed the early external signs of pregnancy, the sight of which brings him a great darkness of understanding regarding his betrothed and the Child she is carrying.

The deep interior anguish of Joseph is seen by Mary and she suffers with him. Within the illogic of external appearances, she is the very cause of his suffering. Even in this first of ordeals, the Mother and the Son are united as the objects of human confusion and seeming contradiction because of their united fiat to the plan of the Heavenly Father's mission of Redemption. The Mother "with Jesus in the womb" suffers silently and offers this intensely, while her just and chaste spouse shares in an early passion of heart caused by God's mysterious designs for human salvation. It is a test of Joseph's faith, a measure of his love. Mary, Woman of Silent Suffering, does not defend herself. She awaits in the pain of silence and potential misjudgment for the Heavenly Father to defend his redemptive plan and his virgin daughter.

The Father does indeed defend her: "But as he considered this, behold, an angel of the Lord appeared to him in a dream, saying, 'Joseph, son of David, do not fear to take Mary your wife, for that which is conceived in her is of the Holy Spirit; she will bear a son, and you shall call his name Jesus, for he will save his people from their sins . . .' When Joseph woke from sleep, he did as the angel of the Lord commanded him, he took his wife, but knew her not until she had borne a son; and he called his name Jesus" (Mt. 1:20- 21,23-24).

All those who are proximate to the Redeemer will have their share in suffering, including the Guardian of the Redeemer. Through his fruitful, exceptional sharing (albeit external), in the redemptive Incarnation and its hidden development during the private years of Jesus of Nazareth, Joseph becomes the spiritual Guardian of all the redeemed. He becomes Patriarch of Patriarchs, spiritual father to Jesus, spiritual father to us all.

Lk. 2:22-38 — Simeon's Prophecy of the Co-redemptrix

The role of the Co-redemptrix is soon after confirmed in prophecy by the power of the Spirit of Truth.

The Virgin Mother, though not truly bound under a law given for an expiation of sin, nevertheless obediently subjected herself to the Mosaic Law. In the Temple she fulfills the duties of ritual purification, offering the "poor offering" of one young pigeon for a holocaust and another for a sin offering. There, too, she offers her male-child to the Lord.

In this great paradox, the Mother and Son, who will offer themselves as the "sin offering" for all humanity at Calvary, enter the Temple humbly and offer a sacrifice for the son who is the redemptive Sacrifice itself. In truth the Mother is offering the "rich offering" of the Lamb, the Paschal Lamb whom the Eternal Father will accept when his "hour" has come; the Lamb who is both Victim and High Priest.

Simeon is most likely not a priest, but rather one of the "anawim," a blessed poor one, faithful to Yahweh and His covenant. Simeon is an old man of prayer and expectation, a simple member of the faithful, a humble voice of the *vox populi*, awaiting the Messiah in order that he may journey to his eternal home in peace.

The Temple is first and foremost a place of sacrifice. All that takes place during the event of the Presentation is a real and mysterious foreshadowing of Calvary, with the same two public persons, Jesus and Mary. Mary offers the child in perfect obedience to the redemptive decrees of God — at the Temple and at Golgotha — effecting a historical sharing in humanity's liberation. She performs the offering of the Child to the Eternal Father, joined by the co-offering of herself for the unified goal of Redemption.

Simeon recognizes the child as the "salvation" (Lk. 2:30) prepared in the presence of all peoples, as "a light for revelation to the Gentiles, and for the glory to thy people Israel" (v. 32). But then the holy Simeon turns his gaze to the Mother of salvation, and prophesies that she too, in virtue of her motherly relation to the sign of contradiction, will experience a life and mission of suffering "with Jesus": "Behold, this child is set for the fall and rising of many in Israel, and for a sign that is rejected — and a sword shall pierce through your own soul, too — that the thoughts of many hearts may be revealed" (Lk. 2:34-35).

If the Sign is rejected, then the Mother of the Sign will be rejected. What mother does not share in the suffering of her son when her son is contradicted? But if her son is the prophesied sign of contradiction, (in relation to which all hearts will be "revealed," either for or against the true Redeemer), then she experiences not merely a moment of pain at the Temple, but a lifetime of pain as the Mother united to the Sign, a mother suffering "with Salvation." No greater sacrifice will ever be asked by the Father of all mankind than the one asked of this Son and Mother, with its defining moment at the tree of Calvary. Yet this sacrifice begins long before. Indeed, the sufferings of the Mother begin before the sufferings of the Son.

From the moment of the Presentation, for a period of over thirty years, the Immaculate Heart painfully ponders the prophecy of Simeon, back and forth on different levels of consciousness and concurrent sorrow. From this moment on, her heart is pierced in anticipation due to the knowledge of the suffering awaiting her innocent Child. She will ultimately share the piercing of his Heart, to which hers is indissolubly united. "They shall look on him whom they have pierced" (Jn. 19:37), and the pierced Heart of Mary will "suffer with" the Pierced Heart of Jesus, from which the blood and water of Redemption is destined to flow.

Notes

[1] St. Bernard of Clairvaux, *Hom. 4*, 8-9; *Opera Omnia*, ed. Cisterc. 4, 1966, 53-54.

[2] John Paul II, *Redemptoris Mater*, 39.

[3] I. de La Potterie, *Maria nel mistero dell'Alleanza*, Genoa, 1988, p. 195 (Eng. trans., *Mary in the Mystery of the Covenant*, 1992).

[4] Blessed Teresa of Calcutta, Personal Interview, Calcutta, August 14, 1993.

[5] St. Irenaeus, *Adversus Haereses*, vol. 3, ch. 22, n. 4; *PG* 7, 959.

[6] St. Ephraem, *Opera Omnia*, ed. Assemani, Rome, 1832, vol. 3, p. 546.

[7] St. Ambrose, *Ep.* 49, n. 2; *PL* 16, 1154 A.

[8] St. Augustine, *De Sancta Virgin. iii.*

[9] St. Thomas Aquinas, *Summa Theologica*, III, Q. 30, a. 1.

[10] The patristic tradition which maintains that the original date of the Annunciation and the original date of Good Friday is the same March 25, seems to confirm the inseparability of the Incarnation from the Redemption. Cf. Tertullian, *Adversus Judaeos*, 8; *PL*, 2, 656 in J. Saward, *The Mysteries of March*, Catholic University of America Press, 1990, p. xv.

[11] F. Ceuppens, *De Mariologia Biblica*, Rome, 1951, p. 201; cf. Manelli, "Mary Coredemptrix In Sacred Scripture," *Mary Coredemptrix, Mediatrix, Advocate: Theological Foundations II*, Queenship, 1996, p. 86.

[12] Cf. Lev. 12:2, 8

[13] Cf. Rt. Rev. Aloys Schaefer, *The Mother of Jesus in Holy Scripture* (trans. from the German by Rt. Rev. Ferdinand Brossart), Frederick Pustet, 1913, p. 186.

Chapter IV

Co-redemptrix Fulfilled

Calvary is the summit of human history, where the drama of God's salvation of man reaches its climax. Every human experience and expression, every action, every thought, every exercise of free will, finds its meaning and fulfillment only through the Cross.

It is at Calvary that we see enacted the fulfillment of the Mother Co-redemptrix, but in a category of human experience that transcends the dignity and efficacy of any other human vocation. At Calvary, the Mother *partakes in the very act of Redemption*, which in turn gives Christian meaning, purpose, and value to every other human act throughout the course of history. For it is by the objective measure of salvation, according to the ultimate meaning of love and truth, that all acts will be weighed.

Jn. 19:25-27: "Woman, behold, your son! . . . Behold, your mother"

Here, the prophecy of Simeon is fulfilled by a sword of sorrow so painful that no other human heart could bear it and live. Only the Immaculate Heart is granted the graces by the Eternal Father to endure the immolation of her Son as Victim for her other spiritual sons and daughters to-be. "Near the cross of Jesus stood his mother . . . When Jesus saw his mother, and the disciple whom he loved standing near, he said to his mother, 'Woman, behold, your son!' Then he said to the disciple, 'Behold, your mother!' And from that hour the disciple took her into his own home (Jn. 19:25-27)."

Jesus, Mary, the tree of the Cross. How entirely supernatural is the Heavenly Father's reversal of Satan's initial victory in the original fall of man (Gen. 3:1-6). At Eden, the original human sin is committed by the First Adam through the intercession of the First Eve at the tree of the forbidden fruit. At Calvary, the original human sin is reversed and redeemed by Jesus, the New Adam[1] through the intercession of Mary, the New Eve at the tree of the Cross. The prophecy of Genesis 3:15 is supernaturally fulfilled at Calvary with the "Woman" and her "seed of victory" crushing the head of Satan and his seed of sin.

This is why the Church's Liturgy sings to God the Father the praises of the New Eve in the mission of the Redemption:

> In your divine wisdom, you planned the Redemption of the human race and decreed that the new Eve should stand by the cross of the new Adam: as she became his mother by the power of the Holy Spirit, so, by a new gift of your love, she was to be

> a partner in his passion, and she who had given him birth without the pains of childbirth was to endure the greatest of pains in bringing forth to new life the family of your Church.[2]

"Woman, behold, your son!" (Jn. 19:26). Woman of Genesis, Woman of Cana, and now, near the end of your maternal crucifixion of heart, you, Woman of Calvary, behold, your son. And behold as well your universal office as Spiritual Mother to all those redeemed here at Calvary, represented by your "new son," the beloved disciple. For you, Mary Co-redemptrix, have suffered "with Jesus" for their ransom, and therefore you shall spiritually nourish and protect them with Jesus, the Redeemer of all peoples, as the new Mother of all peoples.

John Paul II eloquently notes of the Mother's share in the "redemptive love" of her Son and its universal, spiritual fecundity for humanity:

> The Mother of Christ, who stands at the very center of this mystery — a mystery which embraces each individual and all humanity — is given as mother to every single individual and all mankind. The man at the foot of the Cross is John, "the disciple whom he loved." But it is not he alone. Following tradition, the Council does not hesitate to call Mary "the Mother of Christ

> and mother of mankind": since she "belongs to the offspring of Adam she is one with all human beings . . . Indeed she is 'clearly the mother of the members of Christ . . . since she cooperated out of love so that there might be born in the Church the faithful.'"
>
> And so this "new motherhood of Mary," generated by faith, is the fruit of the "new" love which came to definitive maturity in her at the foot of the Cross, through her sharing in the redemptive love of her Son.[3]

But what was the actual price of suffering for Mary Co-redemptrix in order to partake "with Jesus" in the Redemption of the human race and, as a result, to become the spiritual Mother of all peoples?

No human mind or heart can fully comprehend the depth and breadth of this suffering. Popes and poets, musicians and artists have sought to convey the Mother's pain in various creative mediums, from the *Stabat Mater* to the *Pieta*. But all human efforts fail, and the humble are quick to acknowledge the inability to grasp fully the genus of suffering "with Jesus" experienced by Our Lady of Sorrows in order to buy back an entire human race.

The Mother stands near the cross of Jesus amidst the litanies of blasphemies intoned by the onlookers, some recited by the ecclesiastically trained who have condemned him by using a rationalistic exegesis of the Father's Law. Other blasphemies are hurled by common people who ignorantly follow their misguided shepherds. Still more contempt is heaped on her son by those who habitually condemn because of their own fallenness. The Mother hears each and every insult individually. She receives her own direct insults as the condemned's mother, as is still the practice today when someone seeks to inflict pain by directing their insult at a person's mother. Such blasphemies are unintended testimonies to the Co-redemptrix's unity of mission with Jesus.

On the cross, Jesus bleeds, but his Mother cannot stop his bleeding and care for his wounds. On the cross, Jesus cannot find a place to rest his head due to the crown of thorns, but his Mother cannot direct his head. On the cross, Jesus "thirsts" (Jn. 19:28), but the Mother cannot give him drink. On the cross, Jesus confesses in human kenosis, "My God, my God, why hast thou forsaken me?" (Mt. 27:46; Mk. 15:34), but the Mother cannot console her Son.

The Mother shares in the Heart of her Son when he utters from the new tree of the Cross, "Father, forgive them, for they know not what they do" (Lk. 23:34). The Mother also forgives and joins in the petition for the Father's forgiveness, as such is the very purpose of Redemption and Coredemption. And the Mother finds a drop of consolation amidst the ocean of desolation (and a confirmation of their redeeming mission) when she hears the Son declaring to the good thief: "Truly I say to you, today you will be with me in Paradise" (Lk. 23:43).

Finally, with a paradoxical bittersweetness of heart, the Mother hears the words of the Son that he is now departing. He is at the moment of death. He will be taken from her, but their lifelong mission of Redemption has been eternally successful in buying back humanity: "It is consummated" (Jn. 19:30). It is not only finished but fulfilled.

John Paul II describes the intensity of the Immaculate Mother's suffering at this moment as "unimaginable":

> In her, the many and intense sufferings were amassed in such an interconnected way that they were not only a proof of her unshakable faith, but also a contribution to the Redemption of all . . . .It was on Calvary that Mary's suffering, beside the suffering of Jesus, reached such an intensity which can hardly be imagined from a human point of view, but which was mysteriously and supernaturally fruitful for the Redemption of the world. Her ascent of Calvary and her standing at the foot of the cross together with the beloved disciple were a special sort of sharing in the redeeming death of her Son.[4]

Rev. 12 : The Woman Clothed "With the Sun"[5] *and the Dragon*

A final scriptural revelation of the Co-redemptrix is given in the mystical language of the Apocalypse.

The vision of the "woman clothed with the sun" of Revelation 12:1 is introduced by the vision of the Ark of the Covenant within the Temple in Revelation 11:19: "Then God's temple in heaven was opened, and the ark of his covenant was seen within his temple . . . And a great sign appeared in heaven, a woman clothed with the sun, with the moon under her feet and on her head a crown of twelve stars" (Rev. 12:1).

Mary is the New Ark who bears within herself Jesus the Redeemer, who is the New Covenant between divinity and humanity.[6] It is of utmost significance that the Marian image of the New Ark ushers in the last great revelation of the Woman of Scripture in all her glory. She is the Woman of solar and celestial brightness, the Woman who is clothed "with the Sun" in brilliant light and surrounded "with Jesus," the true Son and Light of the world.

The Fathers of the Church and later ecclesiastical writers[7] taught that the Woman of Revelation 12 depicts both Mary and the Church in various ways. But in its first sense, the Woman of Revelation 12 must reveal Mary, for the Immaculate Virgin of Nazareth "brings forth a male child, one who is to rule all the nations with an iron rod" (Rev. 12:5). Jesus is that ruler and Mary alone is his true and natural mother.

The Immaculate alone is the Woman placed in enmity with the serpent in the great parallel texts Genesis 3:15 and Revelation 12, an enmity that leads to and culminates in the cosmic battle for souls depicted in Rev. 12: 13, 17: "And when the dragon saw that he had been thrown down to the earth, he pursued the woman who had born the male child . . . then the dragon was angry with the woman, and went off to make war on the rest of her offspring." The spiritual battle between God's greatest creature and his most evil creature comprises the "bookends" of Sacred Scripture, and depicts a struggle for souls that not only extends through the breadth of the Written Word of God but also the entire course of human history, inclusive of our present hour.

The Co-redemptrix, "with Jesus," battles against the Dragon who wars upon the rest of the Woman's offspring, which is redeemed humanity. With his seed of sin in all its forms, including its contemporary manifestations of abortion, communism, pornography, freemasonry, materialism, secularism, cloning, nuclear war and the like, the Dragon seeks to lure her offspring eternally away from the Woman and her Seed of victory.

The Woman of Revelation 12 is, in diverse though complementary ways, both a "Woman of glory" and a "Woman of suffering."[8] She is a woman of *glory* in so far as she is the woman clothed with the sun and crowned by twelve stars (v. 1), who gives birth to the male-child, ruler of all nations (v. 5). She is a woman of *suffering* in so far as she is the woman with child that "cries out in the pangs of birth, in anguish for delivery" (v. 2) and is at war with the Dragon for "the rest of her offspring" (v. 17).

Both the Woman of glory and the Woman of suffering are in the first sense a revelation of Mary Co-redemptrix. The Virgin Mary is the Woman of glory, clothed with the fullness of grace coming from the Son; crowned with twelve stars as Queen of the Apostles and all creation; and who alone gives birth to Jesus, the male-child, King of all nations. She is also the Woman of Suffering, who on Calvary "cries out in the pangs of birth, in anguish for delivery" in giving mystical birth to us all as spiritual "sons" (Jn. 19:25-27). Her glorification in heaven is not merely a decorative honor in acknowledgment of her human role as the mother of the Savior. It is the fruit of her lifelong sharing in his saving mission, her partaking in his suffering, for glory and suffering are inextricably united in the mission of Redemption (Jn. 13:3).

Mary Co-redemptrix continues to this day to battle the Dragon for souls, a mystical battle that sometimes causes her to weep[9] over the loss of so many of her offspring in our times. She is the Woman of Revelation who "cries out in the pangs of birth, in anguish of delivery" and the Woman of Calvary called to "behold, your son." Both passages are parallel revelations of the same co-redeeming Mother who continues to suffer intensely in order to bring forth disciples in Christ Jesus.[10]

When we scripturally examine the Mother's participation in the accomplishment of Redemption by Jesus Christ, the Word of God elicits a simple and obvious conclusion: the Woman and Mother "with Jesus" from the Annunciation to Calvary uniquely shares in the work of Redemption through which the salvation of the human family is obtained, and at the price of the greatest human suffering imaginable.

The Immaculate Mother, in a way that is shared by no other creature, participates in the "Redemption accomplished" as the Co-redemptrix, and therefore becomes the Mediatrix of all graces,[11] in the order of the "Redemption received."[12] Her acquisition of grace leads to her distribution of grace — from the "Mother to us in the order of grace" (*Lumen Gentium*, 61).

The Testaments of Scripture, Old and New, reveal that a man and a woman "sold" humanity to Satan through sin, and a Man and a Woman "bought back" humanity through suffering. The price paid by the Woman "with Jesus" for our eternal ransom is perhaps best poetically conveyed in the classic verses of the *Stabat Mater*:

At the Cross her station keeping,
Stood the mournful Mother weeping,
Close to Jesus to the last.

Through her heart, His sorrow sharing,
All His bitter anguish bearing,
Now at length the sword has passed.

O how sad and sore distressed
Was that Mother highly blessed
Of the sole-begotten One!

Christ above in torment hangs,
She beneath beholds the pangs
Of her dying, glorious Son.

Is there one who would not weep,
'Whelmed in miseries so deep,
Christ's dear Mother to behold?

Can the human heart refrain
From partaking in her pain,
In that Mother's pain untold?

Bruised, derided, cursed, defiled,
She beheld her tender Child,
All with bloody scourges rent.

For the sins of His own nation
Saw Him hang in desolation
Till His spirit forth He sent.

O sweet Mother! Font of love,
Touch my spirit from above,
Make my heart with yours accord.

Make me feel as you have felt;
Make my soul to glow and melt
With the love of Christ, my Lord.

Holy Mother, pierce me through,
In my heart each wound renew
Of my Savior crucified.

Let me share with you His pain,
Who for all our sins was slain,
Who for me in torments died.

Let me mingle tears with you,
Mourning Him who mourned for me,
All the days that I may live.

By the Cross with you to stay,
There with you to weep and pray,
Is all I ask of you to give.

Virgin of all virgins blest!
Listen to my fond request:
Let me share your grief divine.

Let me to my latest breath,
In my body bear the death
Of that dying Son of yours.

Wounded with His every wound,
Steep my soul till it has swooned
In His very Blood away.

Be to me, O Virgin, nigh,
Lest in flames I burn and die,
In His awful judgment day.

Christ, when you shall call me hence,
Be your Mother my defense,
Be your cross my victory.

While my body here decays,
May my soul your goodness praise,
Safe in heaven eternally.
Amen. (Alleluia.)[13]

Notes

[1]Cf. 1 Cor. 15:22, 45.

[2] *Collection of Masses of the Blessed Virgin*, vol. 1, *Sacramentary*, Catholic Book Publishing, 1992, p. 117; original Latin text in *Collectio Missarum de Beata Maria Virgine* I, Libreria Editrice Vaticana, 1987, p. 49.

[3] John Paul II, *Redemptoris Mater*, 23.

[4] John Paul II, *Salvifici Doloris*, 25.

[5] For an extended commentary on Mary as the Woman of Revelation 12, cf. Matthias J. Scheeben, *Mariology*, Herders, 1947, vol. 1, p. 15; Bernard Le Frois, *The Woman Clothed With The Sun: Individual or Collective*, Orbis Catholicus, Rome, 1954; Paul VI, *Signum Magnum*.

[6] Cf. Chapter II, "Co-redemptrix Foretold."

[7] Cf. Le Frois, *The Woman Clothed with the Sun*, ch. 1, arts. 1, 2, 3; de La Potterie, *Maria nel mistero dell' Alleanza,* p. 258.

[8] Manelli, *Mary Coredemptrix In Sacred Scripture*, p. 99.

[9] For example, the documented weeping Madonna statue at the Church approved apparitions of Our Lady of Akita in Japan, where a wooden statue carved in the image of the Lady of All Nations from Amsterdam wept lacrimations on one hundred and one occasions, cf. T. Yasuda, "The Message of Mary Coredemptrix at Akita and Its Complementarity with the Dogma Movement," *Contemporary Insights on a Fifth Marian Dogma*, Queenship, 2000, pp. 235-249.

[10] Cf. R. Laurentin, *La Vergine Maria*, Rome, 1984, pp. 51-52.

[11] For references to Our Lady's title and function as Mediatrix of all graces, cf. Pius VII, *Ampliatio privilegiorum ecclesiae B.M. Virginis ab agnelo salutatae in coenobio Fratrum Ordinis Servorum B.M. V.*, Florentiae, A.D., 1806; in J. Bourasse, *Summa aurea . . .* ,vol. 7, Paris, 1862, col. 546; Pius IX, Encyclical *Ubi Primum*, 1849; Leo XIII, *Supremi Apostolatus*, 1883 and *Octobri Mense*, 1891; St. Pius X, *Ad Diem Illum*; Benedict XV, Apostolic Letter *Inter Sodalicia*, March 22, 1918; *AAS* 10, 1918, and Mass and Office of Mediatrix of all Graces approved

in 1921; Pius XI, Apostolic Letter *Cognitum Sane*, *AAS* 18, p. 213 and Encyclical *Ingravescentibus Malis, AAS* 29, 1937, p. 380; Pope Pius XII, *Superiore Anno, AAS* 32, 1940, p. 145.; Pius XII, cf. *AAS* 45, 1953 and *Mediator Dei*, 1947; John Paul II, *Redemptoris Mater*, ch. 3, "Maternal Mediation" and in a Papal Address, Rome, October 1, 1997, *L'Osservatore Romano*, English edition, October 8, 1997, p. 11; cf. also A. Robichaud, S.M., "Mary, Dispensatrix of all Graces," *Mariology*, vol. 2, pp. 426-460 and Michael O'Carroll, C.S.Sp., "Still Mediatress of All Graces?," *Miles Immaculatæ* vol. 24 , 1988, pp. 121-122. Usages of the Mediatrix of all graces title during the pontificate of John Paul II number seven and are here included (courtesy of the research of Msgr. Arthur B. Calkins):

1. December 1, 1978, Address to the General Council, Provincial Superiors and Directors of the Italian Institutes of the Congregation of St. Joseph (Giuseppini of St. Leonard Murialdo). n. 3:

> We cannot conclude without addressing the Blessed Virgin, so loved and venerated by Murialdo, who had recourse to her as the Universal Mediatrix of all grace. The thought of Mary returned continually in his letters. In them he inculcated the recitation of the rosary, entrusted his sons with spreading devotion to the Holy Virgin, and stated: "If one wishes to do a little good among the young, one must instill love for Mary in them." The beneficial work carried out by your Founder is the best confirmation of this. So follow his example in this matter too [*Inseg* I (1978) 250; *Talks* 370].

2. August 30, 1980, Address to Young People at Our Lady's Shrine on Mount Roio. n. 3:

> I conclude by entrusting you to the Virgin Mary, to whom St. Bernardine was extremely devoted and

whom, it can be said, he went proclaiming all over Italy every day. Having lost his own mother, he chose Our Lady as his mother and always lavished his affection on her and trusted completely in her. He became the singer of Mary's beauty, it can be affirmed, and preaching her mediation with inspired love, he was not afraid to state: "Every grace that is given to men proceeds from a triple ordained cause: from God it passes to Christ, from Christ it passes to the Virgin, from the Virgin it is given to us."

Turn to her every day with confidence and with love, and ask her for the grace of the beauty of your soul and of your life, of what alone can make you happy [*Inseg* III/2 (1980) 495; *ORE* 648:3].

3. January 17, 1988, Angelus Address, n. 2:

> Another center of Marian devotion worthy of mention is the Church dedicated to Our Lady in Meadi, on the outskirts of Cairo, on the banks of the Nile. The Church seems to have been built in the fifth century, even if, in the course of the centuries and in modern times, it has been modified and restored. It is entrusted to the Coptic-Orthodox Christians, and many pilgrims continuously come to this sanctuary to entrust their intentions to the Mediatrix of all graces [*Inseg* XI/1 (1988) 119; *ORE* 1023:5].

4. April 10, 1988, Homily for Octave of Easter in the Roman parish of Mary, Mother of the Redeemer, n. 7:

> In this Marian Year, your parish, which is placed under the patronage of Mary, Mother of the Redeemer, *Redemptoris Mater*, has an extra reason

> for renewing and strengthening its own devotion towards her, the Mediatrix of all graces, our Advocate with her Son Jesus and the Help of Christians. Call upon her, honor her, draw close to her. She will hear you and will obtain for you whatever good you desire [*Inseg* XI/1 (1988) 863; *ORE* 1036:11].

5. July 2, 1990, Reflection Made at the Shrine of Our Lady of Graces in Benevento, n. 1:

> With loving intuition from ancient times you have been able to grasp the mystery of Mary, as Mediatrix of all graces, because she is the Mother of the very Author of Grace, Jesus Christ. That is why the people of Benevento throughout the ages have turned and continue to turn to her, invoking her not only as "Our Lady of Graces," but often also as "Our Lady of Grace" [*Inseg* XIII/2 (1990) 17; *ORE* 1148:2].

6. September 18, 1994, Angelus Address in Lecce, nn. 1, 3:

> From the city of Lecce, honored by the name of *Civitas mariana*, I raise my prayer to you today, Most Holy Virgin. I do so among this beloved people of Apulia, who venerate you with deep devotion and hail you as the Mother of all Graces. You who go before us on the pilgrimage of faith, accompany the Successor of Peter on today's visit, which is a further step in the "Great Prayer for Italy . . . ."
>
> Watch over each with assiduous care, and pour an abundance of your gifts on all, O Queen without the stain of sin, O Mother of all Graces, O Virgin Mary! [*Inseg* XVII/2 (1994) 344-345; *ORE* 1358:8-9].

7. June 28, 1996, Address to the General Chapter of the Mercedarian Sisters of Charity, n. 4:

> May the Virgin Mary, Mother of Christ and of the Church, invoked with the title "de las Mercedes," assist you and lead you to frequent encounters with her divine Son in the Eucharistic mystery. May she, true Ark of the New Covenant and Mediatrix of all graces, teach you to love him as she loved him. May she also support you with her intercession in the various apostolic works in which you are involved. [*Inseg* XIX/1 (1996) 1638; *ORE* 1451:5]

[12] Theologians seek to categorize both the nature of the Redemption and the precise nature of the Mother's participation in the Redemption with terms such as Redemption "*in actu primo*" or participation in "objective redemption," which refer to the obtaining of the graces of Redemption. This is distinguished from Redemption "*in actu secundo*" or "subjective redemption," which identifies the distribution of the graces of Redemption to humanity.

And yet both the historical act of Redemption by Jesus and Mary at Calvary is an "objective" event, and also the reception of these redemptive graces by members of the human family is likewise "objective," in the sense that it is free from a merely relativistic concept of personal Redemption. Perhaps more true to classical terminology of *in actu primo* and *in actu secundo* and yet more compatible for contemporary understanding would be the terms of "Redemption accomplished" to designate the historical acquisition of grace by Christ and Mary, and "Redemption received" to designate its personal salvific reception by the human family.

[13] *Roman Missal, Lectionary for Mass*, Catholic Book Publishing, 1970, p. 801-802.

Chapter V

The Second Eve

The first Christian pastors and theologians, who were so close to the apex of Christian Revelation when the Word became flesh and died for us, were certainly granted special light by the Spirit of Truth in their preaching and teaching of the Gospel for the early Church. Although none of these on his own can claim an "office" of authority or inspiration, nevertheless taken as a whole and confirmed by the papal office which is led by the Spirit, these early Christian authors (and martyrs in many cases) are rightfully revered in the Church with the titles of "Apostolic Fathers" and "Fathers of the Church."

When the early Fathers turn their gaze to the redemptive Incarnation, they naturally recognize and reverence the role of the Virgin Mother of Jesus in the design of salvation. For failure to recognize the role of the Virgin of Nazareth as part of the salvific plan of the Heavenly Father to bring us our Redeemer would be to reject the obvious — to insinuate that the Son had no mother; that the angel sent by the Father did not come to ask for her free consent; and that she did not morally and physically co-operate to give to the Savior the instrument of salvation, his human nature.

Many of the early Fathers also perceive the saving act of the Redeemer in terms of the teaching of St. Paul that "He has let us know the mystery of his purpose, the hidden plan he so kindly made known in Christ from the beginning to act upon in the fullness of time, that he would bring everything together under Christ, as head" (Eph. 1:9-10). This revelation of Christ in becoming the "new head" of creation, in which all else in creation must now be newly understood, is the patristic concept of *Recapitulation*.

This patristic model of "*recapitulatio*" ("going over again," "summing up") based on the Pauline revelation of Christ as the "new head" ("*re-caput*") becomes the principal model in which the Fathers speak of the Redemption. The Redeemer brings together or "recapitulates" in himself all aspects of the first creation and reconciles everything with the Eternal Father. All creation from the beginning of time is now "gone over again" and "brought together" in Christ, now freed from sin and re-created as a type of "second creation." Through this second creation, God returns to the first plan of creation which was halted by the sin of Adam and restores and unites it in the person of the Redeemer. Since the whole race was lost because of the sin of Adam, first father of the human race, it is necessary that Jesus Christ become man, a second or "New Adam," in order to restore or buy back the human race (cf. Rom. 5:12-20). "'The first man Adam became a living being;' the last Adam became a life-giving spirit" (1 Cor. 15:45). [1]

But if Jesus is the "second" or "New Adam," sent by the Heavenly Father to make right the "wrong" of Adam, what of a second or new "Eve" in this saving process?

Along with the principle of Recapitulation, there is also the complementary and integrated theory of *Recirculation* as taught by the Fathers. The principle of Recirculation teaches that the process of salvation accomplished by Christ, the New Adam, must follow step by step the process of the fall accomplished by Adam, although in an essentially opposite way. If the Eternal Father, therefore, planned a restoration of the human family by using the very same, though opposite, means which led to the loss of Adam (as a manifestation of God's absolute power and glory) then what of the part of the process of the loss of grace enacted by Eve? Does not this divine antithetical parallelism demand a representative in Christian Recirculation for the first Eve, so instrumental in the sin of Adam?

The early Fathers are quick to recognize a new "Mother of the Living" who would reverse and replace the old "Mother of the living" (Gen. 3:20). Within this salvific theology of Recapitulation and Recirculation, they see clearly Mary's crucial role in the plan of salvation, and their testimonies regarding this are the fruit of contemplation, sacrifice, and even martyrdom. She is for them unquestionably the "Second Eve."[2]

The early Christian apologist, St. Justin Martyr († c. 165) is the first to speak of the central role of the Virgin Mary in the divine reversal which leads to salvation. Eve conceived the word from the serpent, and gave birth to "disobedience and death"; Mary's fiat gives birth to the Holy One, who overthrows the evil seed of the serpent and opens the gates to life:

> We know that He, before all creatures, proceeded from the Father by His power and will, . . . and by means of the Virgin became man, in order that the disobedience which began from the serpent might have its undoing in the same way in which it arose. For Eve, being a virgin and undefiled, conceiving the word from the serpent, gave birth to disobedience and to death. The Virgin Mary, however, . . . replied to the Angel Gabriel who announced the joyous news that the Spirit of the Lord would come upon her and that the power of the Most High would overshadow her, and that therefore the Holy One to be born of her would be the Son of God: "Be it done unto me according to thy word." Of her He was born . . . through Whom God overthrows the serpent and angels and men like to the serpent.[3]

The erudite Bishop of Lyons, St. Irenaeus († c. 202) is harkened as the first true Mariologist. St. Irenaeus is the first to teach a complete soteriology of Recirculation between the disobedient virgin Eve who is the "cause of death" for herself and the human race, and the obedient virgin Mary who becomes the instrumental cause of salvation for herself and the whole human race:

> Just as she . . . having disobeyed, became the cause of death for herself and for the entire human race, so Mary . . . being obedient, became the cause of salvation for herself and for the entire human race . . . Thus the knot of Eve's disobedience received unloosing through the obedience of Mary. For what the virgin Eve bound by unbelief, that the virgin Mary unfastened by faith.[4]

The "cause of salvation to herself and the whole human race," constitutes a truly extraordinary profession of Marian Coredemption, written by the "Father of Christian orthodoxy" within the second century of the Church. It is nothing short of an astounding testimony to the Mother's unparalleled role with Jesus in salvation from the ancient Church — a proclamation of the Virgin Mother as a direct instrumental cause in Redemption, which begins, but does not end, with the redemptive Incarnation. [5]

This tribute by St. Irenaeus does not propose Mary as the essential or "formal" cause of salvation, but as an instrumental cause, anti-parallel to Eve's instrumental causality in Adam's formal loss of grace for humanity. As

Eve is completely subordinate to Adam in the "death" of the human race, so too is Mary's instrumental role completely subordinate and dependent upon Jesus Christ, the New Adam. For Christ alone is the formal and ultimate cause of salvation and Recapitulation as "head," the "mighty Word and true man" who "redeemed us by his own blood."[6]

The purity of the teaching of St. Irenaeus professes without question that the Virgin Mary, through her obedient "yes," causes the salvation of the entire human race, which in its first effect applies to her own salvation. Irenaeus further identifies the Virgin Mary as the "advocate" or intercessor for the disobedient virgin, through whom the disobedience of Eve is destroyed:

> It was because of a virgin who was disobedient that man fell, and after his downfall became subject to death. In the same way it is because of a Virgin who was obedient to the word of God that man has been regenerated . . . It was proper and necessary that Adam be restored in Christ, in order that what is mortal be absorbed and swallowed up by immortality; and that Eve be restored in Mary, in order that a Virgin become the advocate of a virgin, and the disobedience of one be obliterated and destroyed by the obedience of the other.[7]

Another early Christian bishop and apologist, St. Melito of Sardis (c. 170) alludes in an Easter Homily to the role of the Virgin Mother in the saving sacrifice of the Son:

> He is the slain lamb,
> He is born of Mary, the fair ewe lamb,
> He is taken from the flock
> And delivered over to immolation . . .
> He rose from the dead and raised man from the depth of the grave. [8]

St. Melito uses here the metaphor of the "lamb," which represents both sacrifice and virginal purity in the Old Testament.[9] When he applies the same metaphor for the Mother as for her Son, the Bishop of Sardis clearly refers to the participation of the Mother in the saving sacrifice of Jesus, the slain lamb of God.[10]

Tertullian († c. 240-250) continues the Eve-Mary Recapitulation model in describing the Virgin's role through whom we "recovered the way to salvation":

> It was by a rival operation that God recovered his image and likeness which had been snatched away by the devil. For into Eve, yet a virgin, had crept the word that was the framer of death. In like manner, into a Virgin was to be introduced the Word of God, the builder-up of life; that by the

> same sex whence had come our ruin might also be recovered the way to salvation. Eve had believed the serpent; Mary believed Gabriel. The fault which the former committed by believing, the latter blotted out by believing. [11]

St. Ephraem († 373), Syrian Deacon and Doctor of the Church who is appropriately named the "Harp of the Holy Spirit," sings of Mary's "paying of the debt" for humanity: "Eve wrote a bill of debt and the Virgin paid the debt." [12] St. Ephraem teaches that we are "reconciled" to God through the Mother of God: "My most holy Mistress, Mother of God and full of grace, . . . Spouse of God through whom we are reconciled to Him."[13] He proclaims that God chose the Blessed Virgin to be "the instrument of our salvation,"[14] and calls her the "price of redemption for captives."[15] He is probably the first to invoke Mary under the specific title of "New Eve."[16]

The prolific Marian author and defender of Nicaea, St. Epiphanius, Bishop of Salamis († 403), succinctly summarizes the same instrumental salvific role of Mary as furnishing the "cause of Life" for the world: "Since Eve brought the cause of death to the human race, through which death entered the world, Mary furnished the Cause of life, through Whom life was produced for us."[17]

In the West, during the fourth century "Golden Age" of patristic literature, St. Ambrose, Doctor and spiritual father of St. Augustine, teaches that the Virgin Mother of

Christ "brought forth redemption for the human race"[18]; that she "bore in her womb the remission of sins";[19] and that she "conceived redemption for all."[20]

St. Ambrose further demonstrates that Mary is the first to be "saved" so as to prepare her to participate in the salvation of all: "Let us not be astonished that the Lord, who came to save the world, began his work in Mary, so that she, by whom the salvation of all was being readied, would be the first to receive from her own child its fruits."[21]

St. Augustine († 430), the monumental Father and Doctor of the Church, expands upon the teachings of St. Ambrose by identifying the Virgin Mary as giving from her flesh "the host" for the sacrifice that regenerates all humanity in the name of all humanity.[22] Augustine also forms his teachings on Mary around the structure of the Second Eve, and the fitting representation of the feminine sex in the redemptive triumph over Satan: "It is a great sacrament that, as death came to us by a woman, life was born to us by a woman; so that in both sexes, feminine and masculine, the devil, being conquered, might be tormented, as he had glorified in the downfall of both. He would not have been adequately punished had both sexes been freed, but we had not been freed by both."[23]

St. Augustine further notes that, "A woman handed the poison to the man who was to be deceived. A woman hands salvation to the man to be restored. A woman, by bringing forth Christ, compensates for the sin of the man deceived by a woman."[24] John Paul II identifies St. Augustine as being the first to refer to the Blessed Virgin as the "co-operatrix" of Redemption.[25]

The "golden mouth" of St. John Chrysostom († c. 407) preaches that, "A virgin expelled us from Paradise; through a Virgin we found eternal life. Through a virgin we were condemned; and through a Virgin we were crowned."[26]

The notable preacher of Ravenna, St. Peter Chrysologus († 450) tells us that "all men merited life through a woman."[27] And Proclus of Constantinople († 446), refers to the Mother of the redeemer as "you who alone carry the Redemption of the world."[28]

Still other Fathers and ecclesiastical writers recognize the doctrine of Mary's unparalleled participation as the Second or New Eve in the work of salvation, such as Gregory Thaumaturgus[29] and St. Cyril of Jerusalem.[30] Theodosus of Ancyra calls her the "Mother of the economy,"[31] and Severien of Gabala refers to her as the "Mother of Salvation."[32]

Ancient Christian liturgies, such as the Coptic, Ethiopian, and Mozarabic liturgies (several of which are still in use today), pray the doctrine of Mary in salvation,[33] manifesting the classic liturgical maxim, "*lex orandi, lex credendi*" ("as we pray, so we believe"). The Armenian liturgy, which dates back to the fifth century, invokes the Mother as "salvatrix" ("one who saves") and "liberatrix" ("one who frees").[34]

These Apostolic and Church Fathers, men of extraordinary faith and wisdom living within the first five hundred years of Christianity, attest in a unified consensus that Mary, the New Eve, through obedience and faith uniquely participates in salvation "with Jesus." With beauty and diversity of expression, the Fathers proclaim that Mary is always central, always instrumental, always an essential part of God's plan "with Jesus" to reverse the sin of Adam and Eve, freely partaking in a redemptive Incarnation that was always ultimately directed to Calvary.

The Fathers cannot be judged upon a modern understanding of Redemption that would explicitly teach the redemptive and co-redemptive role of Jesus and Mary at Calvary under the much later soteriological categories of suffering, satisfaction, merit, and sacrifice. *But if we return to the heart of the meaning of Mary Co-redemptrix, the woman "with Jesus" in the work of salvation, there is no question that the patristic concept of the New Eve teaches the doctrine of Marian Coredemption in its more simplified form. The New Eve is the Woman with Jesus who is the "cause of salvation for herself and the whole human race."*

The faithful testimony of the early patristic age to the doctrine of Mary Co-redemptrix embodied in the New Eve model is succinctly captured by the "Church Father of Scripture," St. Jerome († 420): "Death through Eve; life through Mary."[35]

Notes

[1] For a summary of Recapitulation, Recirculation, and extended citations by the Fathers on the Virgin Mother, cf. Luigi Gambero, *Mary and the Fathers of the Church*, Ignatius Press, 1999, ch. 4 (trans. from Italian original, *Maria nel pensiero dei padri della Chiesa,* Edizione Paoline, 1991).

[2] For an extended treatment and source of relevant citations, cf. J. B. Carol, *De Corredemptione Beatae Mariae Virginis*, Rome, Vaticana, 1950, Pars Secunda, Caput I; L. Riley, "Historical Conspectus of the Doctrine of Mary's Co-redemption," *Marian Studies*, vol. 2, 1951.

[3] St. Justin, *Dialogus cum Tryphone*, ch. 100; *PG* 6, 709-712.

[4] St. Irenaeus, *Adversus Haereses*, vol. 3, ch. 22, n. 4.

[5] For St. Irenaeus, the Incarnation was not sufficient for our salvation without the passion. Cf. Fr. B. De Margerie, S.J., "Mary Coredemptrix In the Light of Patristics," *Mary Coredemptrix Mediatrix Advocate Theological Foundations: Towards a Papal Definition?*, Queenship, 1995, p. 7.

[6] St. Irenaeus, *Adversus Haereses*, vol. 5, ch. 1, n. 1.

[7] St. Irenaues, in J. Barthulot, *Saint Irénée: Démonstration de la Prédication Apostolique, traduite de l'Arménien et annotée*, in R. Graffin and F. Nau, *Patrologia Orientalis*, vol. 12, Paris 1919, pp. 772 et seq.

[8] Melito of Sardis, *Easter Homily*, 71, 11. 513-520.

[9] Cf. for example, Lev. 5:6; Num. 6:14; 7:17.

[10] Cf. O. Perler, *Meliton de Sardes, Sur la Pâque et fragments*, *SC* 123, Paris, ed. du Cerf, 1966, p. 176.

[11] Tertullian, *De Carne Christi*, ch. 17; *PL* 2, 827-828.

[12] St. Ephraem, *On the Institution of the Church*, n. 11, J.T. ed. Lamy, Mechliniae, 1889, t. 3, 978.

[13] St. Ephraem, *Opera Omnia*, ed. Assemani, vol. 3, Rome, 1832, p. 528.

[14] *Ibid.*, p. 607.

[15] *Ibid.*, p. 546.

[16] E. Druwé, "La Médiation Universelle de Marie," *Maria: Études sur la Saint Vierge*, ed. H. du Manoir, vol. 1, Paris, 1949, p. 467.

[17] St. Epiphanius, *Adversus Haereses*, 1. 3, t. 2; *PG* 42, 729.

[18] St. Ambrose, *De Mysteriis*, ch. 3, n. 13; *PL* 16, 410.

[19] St. Ambrose, *De institutione virginum*, ch. 13, n. 81, *PL* 16, 339.

[20] *Ibid.* Note: St. Ambrose's other comments regarding the notion of Co-redemptrix will be treated in the light of Arnold of Chartres' discussion of the subject.

[21] St. Ambrose, Lk II, 17; *ML* 15, 559.

[22] St. Augustine, *Serm. Ined.*, 5, nn. 5, 6; *ML* 46, 832-833; in de Margerie, "Mary Coredemptrix In the Light of Patristics," p. 16.

[23] St. Augustine, *De agone christ.*, ch. 22; *PL* XL, 303.

[24] St. Augustine, *Sermo 51 de concord. Matth. Et Luc.*, n. 2; *PL* 38, 335.

[25] Cf. St. Augustine, *De sancta Virginitate*, 6; *PL* 40, 399; John Paul II, General Audience, April 9, 1997, *L'Osservatore Romano*, English edition, April 16, 1997, p. 7.

[26] St. John Chrysostom, *In Psalmos*, 44; *PG* 55, 193.

[27] St. Peter Chrysologus, *Sermo* 142; *PL* 52, 580.

[28] Proclus of Constantinople, *sermo* 5, art. 3; *PG* 65, 720 C.

[29] St. Gregory Thaumaturgus, *Homilia I in Annuntiatione Sanctae Virginis Mariae*; *PG* 10, 1147.

[30] St. Cyril of Jerusalem, *Catechesis*, 12, n. 15; *PG* 33, 741.

[31] Theodosus of Ancyra, *MG* 77, 393 C.

[32] Severien of Gabala, *MG* 56, 4.

[33] For example, cf. de Margerie, "Mary Coredemptrix In the Light of Patristics," p. 21.

[34] Cf. Laurentin, *Le Titre de Corédemptrice, Etude Historique*, Paris, Nouvelles Editions Latines, 1951, p. 11. The original Armenian term is "Pyrgogh."

[35] St. Jerome, *Epist.* 22, 21; *PL* 22, 408.

Chapter VI

"Holy Redemptrix, Pray For Us"

Just as there is no change in the nature of the unborn child from conception to birth but only the passage of time and growth, so too with the doctrine of Mary Co-redemptrix from its scriptural conception and apostolic gestation through its later patristic development.

As the soteriological understanding of Redemption as the "buying back" of humanity from the bondage of Satan developed, so too in natural and peaceful progression did the understanding of the instrumental role of the stainless Mary in the process of Redemption grow. From the New Eve model, the Fathers and doctors of the Church begin to expand their preaching and teaching of the Mother's redemptive role "with Jesus" from conception to birth, and gradually making its way to Calvary.[1]

The second half of the first millennium begins with a witness from the great Eastern Akathist hymn (c. 525) referring to the Mother of God as the "Redemption": "Hail, Redemption of the tears of Eve."[2]

The Latin poet and hymnist, St. Fortunatus († 600) hails the Blessed Virgin's meritorious causality in the world's salvation as "our only remedy," who by giving birth to God "will wash the world from sin":

> O remarkable Virgin, our only remedy,
> Whom God filled with the wealth of the world,
> You merited to hold your Maker in your womb
> And give birth to God, conceiving in faith.
> By this new birth, you will wash the world from sin.[3]

The seventh century brings the first direct references to the Immaculate One who actually "redeems" with the Redeemer, in partaking in the true "buying back" or "ransoming" of the race of man from the slavery of Satan. Although initially at this period, the references to Mary's part in Redemption refer to her cooperation in giving birth to the Redeemer, by the end of the first millennium, the doctrine develops to include her personal suffering "with Jesus" at Calvary. With the growing awareness of the Redeemer's ransoming of humanity during this century comes the juxtaposed testimonies to the Mother's share in that ransoming.

The Greek word for redemption is "*lutrosis*," which in its ancient meaning denotes a ransom or discharge of a debt. Its patristic meaning conveys an act of deliverance, release, or literally of redemption. Both ancient and patristic Greek meanings are based on the etymological root "*luo*" which refers to a dissolving or loosening. The "buying back" meaning of the Latin, "*redimere*" and the "dissolving a debt" meaning of the Greek "*lutrosis*" are both conveyed in complimentary fashion in these patristic references to the Mother's share in the Redemption.

St. Modestus of Jerusalem († 634), Patriarch of Jerusalem (or "Pseudo- Modestus),[4] refers to the glorious Mother of God through whom "we have been redeemed" (Gk., *lelutrometha*) from bondage to Satan: "O very beautiful dormition of the very glorious Mother of God through whom we have received the remission of our sins (Eph. I, 7) and have been redeemed from the tyranny of the devil."[5]

At the same time, Theodorus Minimus Monremita (c. 7th cent.) likewise exhorts: "May all creatures know the great ransom she offers to God."[6]

St. Andrew of Crete († 740), Archbishop and renowned orator, calls Mary the "Mother of the Redeemer" (*tou Lutrotou*),[7] and says of her: "in you, we have been redeemed from corruption."[8] St. Andrew adds: "All of us have obtained salvation through her."[9]

St. Andrew's illustrious contemporary, St. John Damascene († c. 754-787) Doctor of the Church and one of the last and greatest Greek Church Fathers, re-affirms the Holy Virgin's role in buying back humanity. Damascene teaches that the Blessed Virgin is she, "through whom we were redeemed from the curse,"[10] and that it is Mary, "through whom the whole race of mortals is restored."[11]

The ninth century scholar, Alcuin († 804), Abbot of Tours and inspirer of the Carolingian Renaissance, exclaims of Mary's redemptive role: "The whole world rejoices that it has been redeemed through you."[12]

Alcuin's contemporary in the East, St. Tarasius, Patriarch of Constantinople († 806) calls the Blessed Mother the "payment" for Eve's debt, which reflects the ever-growing understanding of the soteriological price of Redemption: "You [Mary], the payment for the debt of Eve."[13] St. Theodore the Studite († 826), the great monastic reformer, calls Mary the "ransom of the world."[14]

With the contribution of the Byzantine monk, John the Geometer, at the end of the tenth century, a new light of understanding shines upon the *inseparability of the Mother and the Son in the accomplishment of Redemption fulfilled at Calvary.* John Paul II acknowledges this historical breakthrough in the doctrine of Mary Co-redemptrix found in John the Geometer's *Life of Mary*, which the Holy Father confirms:

> This doctrine [of Mary's collaboration in Redemption] was systematically worked out for the first time at the end of the 10th century in the *Life of Mary* by the Byzantine monk, John the Geometer. Here Mary is united to Christ in the whole work of Redemption, sharing, according to God's plan, in the Cross and suffering for our salvation. She remained united to the Son "in every deed, attitude, and wish."[15]

John the Geometer identifies Our Lady as the

"Redemption (*lutrosis*) of the captivity,"[16] and describes her union with Jesus in the entire work of salvation:

> The Virgin, after giving birth to her Son, was never separated from him in his activity, his dispositions, his will . . . When he went away, she went with him, when he worked miracles, it was as if she worked them with him, sharing his glory and rejoicing with him. When he was betrayed, arrested, judged, when he suffered, not only was she everywhere present beside him and even realized especially then his presence, but she even suffered with him . . . Terribly sundered, she would have wished a thousand times to suffer the evils she saw her Son suffering.[17]

John expresses gratitude to Jesus for both his sufferings and for the sufferings of his Mother, which directly lead to a spiritual fruitfulness for humanity: "We give thee thanks for having suffered for us such great evils, and for having willed that your Mother should suffer such great evils, for you and for us . . . ."[18]

Christ gives himself as ransom for us and likewise gives his mother as ransom for humanity at every moment, according to the Geometer, so that Jesus: "should die for us once and she should die for us a thousand times in her will, her heart burning just as for you, so also for those for whom she, as the Father, has given her own Son, knowing him to be delivered from death."[19] John moreover professes that Mary suffered for the Church "as a universal mother."[20]

We must ponder the fact that *well over one thousand years ago, the People of God testified to the spiritual fruitfulness of the Mother's suffering "with Jesus" from the Annunciation to Calvary for our universal ransom*. In this recognition of the countless sufferings of the Mother's heart in the death of her crucified Son is also the recognition of her newly merited role as universal spiritual mother for the Church and for all mankind.

Here, in the tenth century, after nearly a millennium of peaceful gestation, the *explicit doctrine of Mary Co-redemptrix at Calvary is born.*

The "Redemptrix" Title

In a French Psalter which dates back to the tenth century, a litany of saints invokes the petition, "Holy Redemptrix of the world, pray for us."[21] In the beauty of relation between "doctrine" and "title," between the truth conveyed in a doctrine and that selfsame truth being captured in a single word, this petition to the Virgin Mother of Jesus under the title of "Redemptrix" reflects the development of doctrine as testified to by John the Geometer.

The New Eve is always understood by the Fathers as the Virgin Mother who freely and actively participated with and under Jesus, the New Adam in the restoration of grace for the human family. In the early Middle Ages, as the understanding of Redemption becomes more focused on its fulfillment in Christ crucified at Calvary, so too is the Mother's participation at Calvary more recognized and revered. But the same principle of subordinate participation present in the New Eve model is also present in the "Redemptrix" title and doctrine — the Mother participating in a mode of complete creaturely subordination and dependency upon her divine Son the Redeemer, who alone has the power to reconcile earth to heaven.

This tenth century petition does not end with, "Holy Redemptrix of the world, have mercy on us," which would have inferred an erroneously parallel or competitive relation to the one divine Redeemer, but rather "Holy Redemptrix of the world, pray for us." It asks her intercession in the sense of all Christian petitions seeking the powerful intercession of human saints. Was it rash for our medieval brothers and sisters to call Mary the "Redemptrix?"[22] Properly understood, it was no more rash to call Mary the "Redemptrix" than for the Church to call Mary the "Mediatrix."

The title of Redemptrix conveys the general doctrine of Marian Coredemption, the understanding of which grows as her role at Calvary is better understood. "Redemptrix" (like the later "Co-redemptrix"), is used in the context of complete and total subordination to Christ Jesus, divine Redeemer and Lord of all. No more than the title "New Eve" threatens the primacy of the "New Adam" in the teachings of the Fathers, does "Redemptrix" threaten the primacy of Christ the "Redemptor" among the Medievals. Just as we invoke the Mother of Jesus as "Mediatrix" (*Lumen Gentium*, 62), and not "co-Mediatrix," with the proper understanding of her complete subordination as creature to Jesus the "one Mediator" (1 Tim.2:5),[23] so in the same way it is perfectly legitimate and theologically orthodox to call Mary the "Redemptrix" within the same ecclesial understanding of total subordination to the Redeemer.

Both in doctrine and in title, Marian Coredemption greatly advances during the tenth through fourteenth centuries, a period which prepares the way for the further Mariological development of Mary "Co-redemptrix." References to the Mother as "Redemptrix" which honor Our Lady's giving birth to the Redeemer continue alongside a more explicit testimony to her suffering "with Jesus" at Calvary.

The "Virgin Mother of God gives birth as our Redemptrix" writes an anonymous eleventh century author.[24] The great St. Peter Damian († 1072), Cardinal and Doctor of the Church, calls the Church to give thanks to the Mother of God, after God himself, for our Redemption:" ...we are debtors to the most blessed Mother of God, and . . . after God we should thank her for our redemption."[25]

St. Anselm († 1109), perhaps the greatest early scholastic theologian and philosopher, speaks of the Redemption as a unified victory of Mother with Son:

"What I say worthily I will refer to the Mother of God and of my Lord through whose fecundity I, a slave, have been redeemed, through whose birth I am exempt from eternal death."[26] St. Anselm further declares: "Thou art the salvation of sinners, O Son, and thou, O Mother,"[27] and also: "Through thee we have access to the Son Who redeemed the world through thee."[28]

Eadmer of Canterbury († 1124), companion to St. Anselm, is one of the first to speak of Our Lady's "*merit*" in connection with the Redemption, and invokes Blessed Mary as the "Reparatrix." The Reparatrix term is basically an equivalent term to Redemptrix, but with an emphasis upon the restoring or repairing of the relationship between God and man. Reparatrix will be used in reference to the Mother by Pope St. Pius X some nine hundred years later.[29] Eadmer teaches that Mary "merited to become in a most worthy manner the Reparatrix of the lost world"[30]; and that, "Just as God in making everything by His power is the Father and Lord of all things, so the Blessed Mary in repairing everything by her merits is the Mother and Lady of all things."[31]

St. Bernard and Arnold of Chartres: Co-suffering and "Co-crucified"

A monumental contribution to the story of Mary Co-redemptrix comes with the insights of the great St. Bernard of Clairvaux († 1153), arguably the most significant figure of the twelfth century, and his disciple, Arnold of

Chartres († 1160).

St. Bernard, who has sometimes been called "the last of the Church Fathers," is the first to teach of Mary's "offering" of Jesus as the divine victim to the Heavenly Father for the reconciliation of the world. St. Bernard's teachings are in the context of Mary's offering of Jesus at the Presentation of the Temple (and not yet at Calvary): "O hallowed Virgin, offer thy Son; and present anew to the Lord this Fruit of thy womb. Offer for our reconciliation this Victim, holy and pleasing to God. With joy, God the Father will receive this oblation, this Victim of infinite value."[32]

The Abbot of Clairvaux is also the first to refer to the "compassion"[33] of Our Lady, a term which etymologically comes from the Latin "cum" (with) and "passio" (suffering or receiving), and therefore refers to her "co-suffering" or "suffering with" Jesus. According to Bernard, the Virgin Mother welcomes the "price of Redemption"[34]; stands at "Redemption's starting point"[35]; and "liberates prisoners of war from their captivity."[36]

In addition, St. Bernard is the first theologian and Doctor of the Church to preach that Mary provided "satisfaction" for the disgrace and ruin brought about by Eve: "Run, Eve, to Mary; run, mother to daughter. The daughter answers for the mother; she takes away the opprobrium of the mother; she makes satisfaction to Thee, Father, for the mother . . . O woman singularly to be venerated . . . Reparatrix of parents."[37]

The pivotal Mariologist, Arnold of Chartres, St.

Bernard's renowned disciple, can rightly be considered the first author who formally expounds the explicit doctrine of Mary Co-redemptrix at Calvary. While two centuries earlier, John the Geometer had referred to the suffering of Mary with the crucified Jesus, Arnold specifies *that it is Jesus and Mary who together accomplish the Redemption through their mutual offering of the one and the same sacrifice to the Father.* The French abbot tells us: "Together they [Christ and Mary] accomplished the task of man's redemption . . . both offered up one and the same sacrifice to God: she in the blood of her heart, He in the blood of the flesh . . . so that, together with Christ, she obtained a common effect in the salvation of the world."[38]

In a theological and terminological breakthrough, Arnold states that Mary is "co-crucified" with her Son[39] at Calvary, and that the Mother "co-dies" with him.[40] In response to objections first raised by Ambrose that Mary did not suffer the passion, was not crucified like Christ, and did not die as Christ died at Calvary, Arnold responds that Mary experienced "com-passion" or "co-suffering" (using the term of his master, Bernard) with the passion of Christ: "what they did in the flesh of Christ with nail and lance, this is a co-suffering in her soul."[41] Further, Arnold explains that Mary is in fact "co-crucified" in her heart with Jesus crucified,[42] and that the Mother "co-dies" with the death of her son. Mary "co-died with the pain of a parent."[43]

Arnold concludes that the Mother of the Redeemer does not "operate" redemption at Calvary, but rather "co-operates" in Redemption, and to the highest degree.[44] It is the love of the Mother that co-operates in a unique way at Calvary, in a way most favorable to God: "[On Calvary] the Mother's love co-operated exceedingly, in its own way, to render God propitious to us."[45]

How truly extraordinary was the contribution of Bernard and Arnold. The Mother's role in Redemption is affirmed by Bernard in the terms, *offering*, *satisfying*, and *compassion*. Her role at Calvary is proclaimed by Arnold in the terms *co-crucified*, *co-dying*, *co-operating*. These testimonies can be likened, in their theological insight and maturity, to contemporary testimonies to Mary Co-redemptrix by popes of the twentieth and twenty-first centuries. The doctrine and title development of the Co-redemptrix story, exemplified in an extraordinary way during this late patristic and early medieval period, will soon bear even greater fruit in bringing forth the singular title which most clearly expresses the Mother's unique collaboration with and under Jesus in the Redemption.

Notes

[1] For a more extensive treatment of the medieval and modern history of the title of Mary Co-redemptrix and Marian Coredemption, cf. Carol, *De Corredemptione*; R. Laurentin, *Le Titre de Corédemptrice*; G. Roschini, *Maria Santissima Nella Storia Della Salvezza*, vol. 2, pp. 171-232; L. Riley, "Historical Conspectus of the Doctrine of Mary's Co-redemption." Numerous citations contained in this work were located in these extended treatments. Note: The references found in the Laurentin article illustrate the author's exceptional historical scholarship, but much of the commentary on the development of Marian Coredemption in regards to the usages of "Redemptrix" and "Co-redemptrix" does not appear substantiated by his own excellent sources (cf. note 23 from this chapter, and Chapter VIII, note 6).

[2] *Akathist Hymn*, Strophe 1; *PG* 92, 1337 A.

[3] St. Fortunatus, *In laudem S. Mariae Virginis et Matris Domini*, verse 119-125; *PL* 88, 284.

[4] For controversy over authenticity of authorship, cf. M. Jugie, "Deux homélies patristiques pseudépigraphes. Saint Athanase sur l'Annonciation et saint Modeste de Jérusalem sur la Dormition," *Echos d'Orient,* 30, 1941-2, pp. 283-289, and Dom. B. Capelle, "Témoignage de la liturgie . . . ," *Bulletin de la société française d'études mariales,* 7, 1949, pp. 40-41, n. 16.

[5] *Enconium in B. Virginem,* VII; *PG* 86, 3293 B.

[6] Theodorus Minimus Monremita, *s. in annunciatione,* t. 8, in A. Ballerini, *Sylloge,* Paris, Lecoffre, 1857, t. 2, p. 229.

[7] St. Andrew of Crete, *Canon in Nativ.*, ode 4; *PG* 97, 1322 B.

[8] *Ibid.*, ode 5; *PG* 97, 1322 C.

[9] St. Andrew of Crete, *Canon in B. Annae conceptionem*; *PG* 97, 1307.

[10] St. John Damascene, *Homilia in Annuntiationem B. V. Mariae*; *PG* 96, 657. Laurentin attributes this reference to "Pseudo-John Damascene," cf. Laurentin, *Le Titre de Corédemptrice*, p. 59.

[11] St. John Damascene, *Homilia I in Nativitatem B. V. Mariae*; *PG* 96, 661.

[12] Alcuin, *s. de Nativ.*; *PL* 101, 1300 D.

[13] St. Tarasius, *Sermo in Praes.*, IX; *PG* 98, 1492 A.

[14] St. Theodore the Studite, *Triodium Dominicae abstinentiae*, ode y, cited in A. Ballerini, *Sylloge*, t. 2, p. 229, note c.

[15] John Paul II, General Audience, Oct. 25, 1995, n. 2; *L'Osservatore Romano*, English edition, Nov. 1, 1995, p. 11.

[16] John the Geometer, *S. on the Annunciation*; *PG* 106, 846 A.

[17] John the Geometer, *Life of Mary* as found in A. Wenger, A.A., "L'Assomption," *Études Mariales*, BSFEM, 23, 1966, 66, as quoted in English by M. Carroll, C.S.Sp., *Theotokos*, Michael Glazier, p. 204.

[18] *Ibid.*, Wenger, *L'Assomption*, p. 406.

[19] *Ibid.*

[20] *Ibid.*

[21] *Litanies des saintes*, in a Psalter of French origin preserved in the chapter library of the Cathedral of Salisbury, Parchment 173, fol. in double columns, 0.39x0.32 m. Manuscript number l80, fol. 171 v., b. Edited by F.E. Warren, "An Unedited Monument of Celtic Liturgy" in *Celtic Review*, 9, 1888, pp. 88-96.

[22] Cf. Laurentin, *Le Titre de Corédemptrice*, p. 12. Fr. Laurentin refers to Redemptrix as a "rash title," and calls shortened versions of "Mary is Redemption" and "she redeems; she is redemptrix" as "disconcerting" (p. 13). Laurentin does defend the legitimacy of "Redemptrix" as denoting an "equivocal affirmation" of more ancient expressions of "Mary redeems" ("from *Maria redemit* to *Maria Redemptrix*, the nuance is without importance," p. 12), and that these terms convey an all together different meaning by the Fathers for Mary than that which is unique for Christ the Redeemer in paying the price for sin. But he nonetheless fails to validate the participatory dimension of Mary in the very act of Redemption beyond the Incarnation, as contained in these later references to Mary's role in Redemption, which are but a natural development of those ancient expressions of "New Eve" and the

principle of Recapitulation in which the New Eve does share instrumentally though subordinately in the saving process with the New Adam in salvation, and in the necessary reversal of Eve's participation with Adam in sin. To accept the patristic model of New Eve with its obvious instrumental causality in salvation, and then to exclude any true sharing on the part of Mary in the later soteriology of Redemption as spoken of in the tenth through fourteenth centuries is to negate the latter as a true and solid development of the former.

Redemption is in fact to pay the price for someone's liberation, and this price is paid in source by Jesus Christ, New Adam, "Redemptor," and by participation by the Mother of Jesus, New Eve, "Redemptrix" (and later, Co-redemptrix). This is God's deliberate plan of salvation, so foundational to the entire Recapitulation theory of saving the human race by using the very same means through which it was lost – the free act of a man and a woman – and thus manifesting God's omnipotence and glory. It is only when we *a priori* reject any legitimate human participation in the Redemption accomplished by Christ, a position which runs contrary to contemporary magisterial references to true Marian participation in Redemption as found, for example, in *Lumen Gentium*, 57, 58, 61, or *Salvifici Doloris*, 25 (Mary's sufferings at Calvary were a "contribution to the Redemption of all,") that one is then forced to conclude that these "Mary-redemption" references run the danger of becoming a parallel or rival to the Redemption achieved by Christ. They constitute no such threat, and the context of their usage during the pre-scholastic, scholastic, and post-scholastic periods (as they did in more concise forms in the patristic age), manifest a true sharing by Mary in the Redemption wrought by Christ.

[23] Cf. *Lumen Gentium*, 60, 62.

[24] Inscription with an illustration on the nativity, Ms. 123 of the *Bibliotheca Angelica*, Rome, fol. 29v.

[25] St. Peter Damian, *Sermo 45 in Nativitate Beatissimae Virginis Mariae*; *PL* 144, 743.

[26] St. Anselm of Canterbury, *Oratio* 52; *PL* 158, 953 C-954 A.

[27] St. Anselm, *Oratio* 51; *PL* 158, 951.

[28] St. Anselm, *Oratio* 54, *PL* 158, 961. Some authors consider this a quote from "Pseudo- Anselm," cf. A. Wilmart, *Revue benedictine,* 36, 1924, pp. 52-71.

[29] Pius X, *Ad Diem Illum*, 12.

[30] Eadmer of Canterbury, *Liber de Excellentia Virginis Mariae*, c. 9; *PL* 159, 573.

[31] *Ibid.*, c. 11; *PL* 159, 578.

[32] St. Bernard of Clairvaux, *Sermo 3 de Purificatione Beatae Mariae*; *PL* 183, 370.

[33] St. Bernard; *PL* 183, 438 A.

[34] St. Bernard, *Homil. 4 sup. Missus est*; *PL* 183, 83 C.

[35] St. Bernard, *Sermon des 12 étoiles*; *PL* 183, 430 C.

[36] *Ibid.*; *PL* 183, 430 D; *Homil. 4 sup. Missus est*; cf. Laurentin, *Le Titre de Corédemptrice*, p. 14 ff.

[37] St. Bernard, *Homilia 2 super Missus est*; PL 183, 62.

[38] Arnold of Chartres, *De Laudibus B. Mariae Virginis*; *PL* 189, 1726-1727.

[39] Arnold of Chartres; *PL* 189, 1693 B.

[40] *Ibid.*

[41] Cf. Laurentin, *Le Titre de Corédemptrice*, p. 15, note 51; "quod in carne Christi agebant clavi et lancea, hoc in ejus mente compassio naturalis"; *PL* 189, 1731 B.

[42] *Ibid.*, p. 15, note 52; "concrucifigebatur affectu"; *PL* 189, 1693 B.

[43] *Ibid.*, p. 15, note 53; "parentis affectu commoritur"; *PL* 189, 1693 B

[44] *Ibid.*, p. 15, note 54; "co-operabatur...plurimum"; *Tractatus de septem verbis Domini in cruce*, tr. 3; *PL* 189, 1695 A.

[45] Arnold of Chartres, *Tractatus de septem verbis Domini in cruce*; tr. 3; PL 189, 1694.

Chapter VII

"My Son and I Redeemed the World"

During the thirteenth and fourteenth centuries, a providential blend of theologians, saints, and mystics continue the fruitful development of the doctrine of Mary Co-redemptrix.

The mystical dimension begins to play an important role in this and in later periods of Coredemption's doctrinal development, with great spiritual figures such as St. Catherine of Siena and St. Bridget of Sweden contributing to the harmony between theology and spirituality within the Church. The Holy Spirit can and does use his prophetic gifts through chosen souls as lights to guide the great bark of Tradition and theology upon a particular path of doctrinal development.

What the revelations received by St. Margaret Mary Alacoque are to the development of the doctrine of the Sacred Heart of Jesus, and the revelations of St. Faustina Kowalska to Divine Mercy in our own times,[1] the *Revelations* of St. Bridget are to the medieval progress of the doctrine of Mary Co-redemptrix. For the *Revelations* convey to us in the words of the Blessed Mother herself that, "*My son and I redeemed the world*."[2]

The Immaculate One's compassion and its fruitfulness at Calvary is championed by the prominent theologian, Richard of St. Lawrence († 1230), who speaks of the Mother's reconciling of the guilty in her "communion with" the passion of Christ: "What the Son bestowed upon the world by His passion, the Mother bestowed upon the world by her communion with it, reconciling the guilty and the sinners by her co-passion, after having obtained the Redemption of the whole world through her giving birth to the Redeemer."[3] He goes on to speak of Our Lady's suffering with Jesus at Calvary: "Her tears were mingled with [His] perspiration and tears, with the water and the blood that trickled from the wounds of her Son, in order to blot out the stains of souls."[4]

The greatest of all Franciscan theologians, St. Bonaventure († 1274), promulgates in his own expressions the breakthroughs of St. Bernard and Arnold regarding the Mother's Coredemption. The Seraphic Doctor shows that the New Eve doctrine of Coredemption taught by the Church Fathers is fulfilled in Jesus and Mary as the "repairers" of the human race: "Just as they [Adam and Eve] were the destroyers of the human race, so these [Jesus and Mary] were its repairers."[5]

St. Bonaventure explicitly relates the patristic principles of Recapitulation and Recirculation[6] to the suffering of Mary at Calvary for our Redemption. Mary "bought us," and she "paid the price"[7] with Jesus on the cross: "That woman (namely Eve), drove us out of Paradise and sold us; but this one (Mary) brought us back again *and bought us.*"[8] The Mystical Father of Franciscan theology declares that Mary "also merited reconciliation for the entire human race"[9]; that she "co-offered" the divine victim on Calvary;[10] and she offered "satisfaction" for our sins.[11]

Contemporaneous with the Franciscan contribution to Marian Coredemption comes a most significant Dominican contribution from St. Albert the Great († 1280), mentor to St. Thomas Aquinas and Church Doctor in his own right. St. Albert teaches that the Virgin Mary exercised the "principle of association or participation"[12] with Christ in the Redemption of the human race, and that she "participated in all of his same acts."[13]

"Pseudo-Albert" soon follows the Great Albert and elaborates and systematizes the same "*principium consortii*" of Mary in Redemption in the renowned work, *Mariale.*[14] In this work, the author calls Mary the "co-helper of the redemption" (*co-adjutrix redemptionis*)[15]; affirms that at Calvary, Mary the New Eve helped Christ "to regenerate the human race to the life of grace"[16]; and speaks eloquently of her compassion as the adjutrix or "helpmate" of Redemption at Golgotha:

> To her [Mary] alone was given this privilege, namely, a communication in the Passion; to her the Son willed to communicate the merit of the Passion, in order that He could give the reward; and in order to make her a sharer in the benefit

> of Redemption, He willed that she be a sharer in the penalty of the Passion, in so far as she might become the Mother of all through re-creation even as she was the adjutrix of the Redemption by her co-passion. And just as the whole world is bound to God by His supreme Passion, so also it is bound to the Lady of all by her co-passion.[17]

Mary uniquely participates in the Passion. Mary uniquely merits in its accomplishment. The world is uniquely bound to her, in virtue of her co-passion, Mother of us all through our re-creation.

At the beginning of the fourteenth century, the great Franciscan champion of the Immaculate Conception, Bl. John Duns Scotus (†1308) uses the title, "Redemptrix" in recording a typical scholastic objection to the Immaculate Conception and Mary's role in Redemption, which Duns Scotus then refutes.[18]

At this historical point enters the mystical contribution of St. Bridget of Sweden († 1373). The *Revelations*, the written record of a series of visions and prophecies granted to St. Bridget by Jesus and Mary, are highly regarded and reverenced by the Church during the Middle Ages, including a large number of popes, bishops, and theologians.[19] The revealed words spoken by both Jesus and His Mother regarding Our Lady's coredemptive role are truly significant in the development of the Co-redemptrix doctrine, as they will influence numerous theologians during the seventeenth century "Golden Age" of Coredemption, some three hundred years later.

The Mother of Sorrows reveals in these prophetic visions through St. Bridget that "*My son and I redeemed the world as with one heart.*"[20] Jesus confirms the same truth in his own words: "*My Mother and I saved man as with one Heart only, I by suffering in My Heart and My Flesh, she by the sorrow and love of her Heart.*"[21] It is difficult to argue with the supernatural testimony from such a Church-sanctioned and revered prophecy regarding the role of Mary Co-redemptrix — a testimony from the lips of the Redeemer and the Co-redemptrix themselves. The medievals, as a whole, did not.

The Rhineland Mystic, John Tauler († 1361) offers his own theological and mystical contribution to Mary Co-redemptrix. Like no other author before him, this Dominican theologian articulates with precision the *sacrificial offering* of the Mother at Calvary.

In the teachings of Tauler, the Mother of Jesus offers herself with Jesus as a living victim for the salvation of all,[22] and the Eternal Father accepted this oblation of Mary for the salvation of the entire human race: "God accepted her oblation as a pleasing sacrifice, for the utility and salvation of the whole human race . . . so that, through the merits of her sorrows, she might change God's anger into mercy."[23] In the natural progression of the New Eve patristic Recapitulation brought to its fullness at Calvary, Blessed John speaks of the sorrow the Mother plucked from the tree of the cross in order to redeem humanity with her Son: "Just as Eve, boldly plucking from the tree of the knowledge of good and evil, destroyed men in Adam, so thou hast taken sorrow upon thyself from the tree of the cross, and with thy suffering sated, thou has redeemed men together with thy Son."[24]

Addressing Our Lady, Tauler tells us of Mary's foreknowledge of her co-suffering with Jesus, in which she would share in all his redemptive merits and afflictions: "He foretold to thee [Mary] all thy passion whereby He would make thee a sharer of all His merits and afflictions, and thou would co-operate with Him in the restoration of men to salvation . . . ."[25]

We close this fertile thirteen and fourteenth century period of Marian Coredemption, so richly fed by a providential blend of theologian and mystic, with the witness of the "mystic of mystics," St. Catherine of Siena († 1380). The great Church Doctor and Co-patroness of Europe calls the Blessed Mother the "Redemptrix of the human race" both in virtue of giving birth to the Word and for the sorrow of "body and mind" that Our Mother suffers with Jesus: "O Mary . . . bearer of the light . . . Mary, Germinatrix of the fruit, Mary, Redemptrix of the human race because, by providing your flesh in the Word, you redeemed the world. Christ redeemed with His passion and you with your sorrow of body and mind."[26]

Notes

[1] For example, the influence of St. Faustina's revelations to the development of the encyclical, *Dives in Misericordia*, or the liturgical development of the Feast of Divine Mercy.

[2] St. Bridget, *Revelationes*, L. I, c. 35, ed. Rome, ap. S. Paulinum, 1606, p. 56b.

[3] Richard of St. Lawrence, *De laudibus Beatae Mariae Virginis*, 1. 3, c. 12; inter *Opera Sancti Alberti Magni*, ed. Vivès, vol. 36, p. 158.

[4] Cf. C. Dillenschneider, *Marie au service de notre Rédemption*, Haguenau, 1947, p. 246.

[5] St. Bonaventure, *Sermo 3 de Assumptione*; *Opera Omnia*, ed. Aquas Claras, vol. 9, p. 695.

[6] While some theologians prefer to use the term of Recapitulation for the Adam-Christ parallel and Recirculation for the Eve-Mary parallel, there is also a danger in restricting the Eve-Mary parallel to the soteriological dimension of Recirculation, and in doing so to infer that the Virgin Mother did not have an active though subordinate role with Christ in the Recapitulation, but only with Christ in the antithetical reversal aspect of the restoration. Mary actively participates in both patristic concepts of Recapitulation and Recirculation, as evident in St. Irenaeus: "Adam had to be Recapitulated in Christ, so that death might be swallowed up in immortality, and Eve [had to be Recapitulated] in Mary, so that the Virgin, having become another virgin's advocate, might destroy and abolish one virgin's disobedience by the obedience of another virgin" (*Proof of Apostolic Preaching* 33, SC 62, pp. 83).

[7] Cf. St. Bonaventure, *De donis Spiritus Sancti*, collatio 6, n. 5/17; *Opera Omnia*, ed. Claras Aquas, 1882-1902, vol. 5, p. 484.

[8] St. Bonaventure, *de don. Sp*. 6; 14.

[9] St. Bonaventure, *In III Sent.*, dist. 4, art. 3, quaest. 3, concl.; *Opera Omnia*, ed. Claras Aquas, vol. 3, p. 115.

[10] Cf. St. Bonaventure, *De donis Spiritus Sancti*, collatio 6, n. 17; *Opera Omnia*, vol. 5, p. 486.

[11] *Ibid.*, collatio 6, n. 16.

[12] St. Albert the Great, *Comment. In Matt.* I, 18; *Opera Omnia,* vol. 37, p. 97; cf. Roschini, *Maria Santissima Nella Storia Della Salvezza*, vol. 2, p. 184.

[13] *Ibid.*

[14] Pseudo-Albert, *Mariale super Missus est*; *Opera Omnia.*

[15] *Ibid.*, q. 42, 4. t. 37, 81.

[16] *Ibid.*, 29, 3.

[17] *Ibid.*, q. 150.

[18] Bl. Duns Scotus, Ms. Ripoll. 53, Barcelone, L. III, dist. 3, q. 1 in C. Balić, O.F.M., *Theologiae marianae elementa*, Sibenici, typ. Kačić, 1933, pp. 211, 28-31.

[19] Cf. St. Bridget, *Revelationes*, ed. Rome, ap. S. Paulinum, 1606.

[20] St. Bridget, *Revelationes*, L. I, c. 35.

[21] St. Bridget, *Revelationes*, IX, c. 3.

[22] John Tauler, *Sermo pro festo Purificat. B. M. Virginis*; *Oeuvres complètes*, ed. E. P. Noël, Paris, vol. 5, 1911, p. 61.

[23] *Ibid.*, vol. 6, pp. 253-255.

[24] *Ibid.*, p. 256.

[25] *Ibid.*, p. 259.

[26] St. Catherine of Siena, *Oratio* XI, delivered in Rome on the day of the Annunciation, 1379 in *Opere*, ed. Gigli, t. IV, p. 352.

Chapter VIII

"You Would Become Co-redemptrix"

While the more complete story of Mary Co-redemptrix is being told by medieval theologians and saints, so too the liturgical hymns of the time begin to sing its truth. Between the fourteen and fifteen centuries the title of "Co-redemptrix" makes its first appearance in a liturgical hymn.

Her titles are her functions, and thus, as the medieval mind achieves greater clarity regarding the Mother's salvific function with Jesus, it is appropriate that the title, "Co-redemptrix" which best captures the function of Mary's share in Redemption, would be sung in the public prayer of the Church.

Two stanzas of a fourteenth-fifteenth century Salzburg liturgical hymn, entitled *Plainchant to the Blessed Virgin holding in her lap her Son, taken down from the Cross*, record perhaps the earliest known use of the term, "Co-redemptrix":

> Good, sweet and kind,
> Absolutely worthy of no grief;
> If you would root out mourning from here

As one suffering with the redeemer,
For the captured transgressor
You would become co-redemptrix

Then I see that one ought not so much to grieve with
My sad mother as
I see that I ought to pay thanks
To you, my redemptrix,
Who deigns to free
Me from the hand of the enemy.[1]

We see in this hymn the use of both "Co-redemptrix" and "Redemptrix" titles. The Redemptrix title, used at least four centuries earlier than Co-redemptrix, certainly conveys the same subordinate role and function of the Immaculate Virgin. But with the terminological breakthroughs of St. Bernard,[2] Arnold of Chartres,[3] and Pseudo-Albert,[4] we see how the prefix, "co," can assist in emphasizing the distinction between the entirely necessary and foundational accomplishment of the Redemption by Jesus Christ, from the exalted participation of the Immaculate Mother in the Redemption.

The Redemptrix title will continue to be used in a doctrinally orthodox way within the Church for several centuries more,[5] juxtaposed with a gradual increase in the use of Co-redemptrix. But "Redemptrix" will gradually give way to the title which accents the Mother's subordination and dependency, etymologically conveyed in "Co-redemptrix."

In the middle of the fifteenth century, the renowned Dominican reformer and Archbishop of Florence, St. Antoninus († 1459) elaborates the insights of St. Albert and Pseudo-Albert. He explains Mary's unique participation in the merit of Christ's Passion, which leads her to become the "Mother of all through re-creation":

> It was Mary alone to whom was given the privilege of communication in the Passion. That He might be able to bestow upon her a reward, the Son willed to communicate to her the merit of the Passion; and also that He might make her a sharer of the benefit of Redemption, to the extent that, as she was adjutrix of the Redemption by her co-passion, so also she might become the Mother of all through re-creation."[6]

St. Antoninus calls Mary the "Redemptrix of lost man" who "led him to the heavenly kingdom."[7] In addition, he testifies to the Blessed Virgin's spiritual motherhood of humanity: As a result of her coredemptive suffering in the Passion, she consequently begets us in the spiritual order: "... the Blessed Virgin begot us and gave birth to us, in her co-suffering the bitterest sorrows with her Son"[8]; and further: "... the Mother of mercy helped (*adjuit*) the Father of mercies in the work of the highest mercy, and she bore with [Christ] the suffering of the Passion."[9]

The Co-redemptrix first suffered with the Savior to obtain the spiritual milk of sanctifying grace with which, in turn, to nurse her spiritual children. The popes of the nineteenth and twentieth century will later teach with magisterial authority the truth of Our Lady's mediation of all graces as a fruit of her Coredemption.[10]

Although the late fifteenth and sixteenth centuries experience a general reduction in Marian theology, nonetheless three notable authors of this period make significant contributions.

The French author, Alain de Varènes (c. 1521), calls the Blessed Virgin the "Co-redemptrix" for perhaps the first time in the context of a theological treatise. He uses the title as part of a profound theological articulation of the Mother's unique cooperation in reconciling man to God:

> Therefore most Holy Mary, cooperated with her Son, and met a similar fate of action, bringing it about with her love, has made both one, having broken down the barrier of hostility . . . in imitation of her Only Begotten Son, breaking down the barrier of the garden, which is hostility, by abolishing in the flesh of her Only-begotten Son the law of commandments and ordinances that he might create in himself one new man in place of the two, and in so doing making peace, and that he might

> reconcile all in one body to God through the cross of her Son, thereby bringing hostility to an end in the Lord Jesus and, in a certain way, in herself as co-redemptrix (as they wish), preaching "peace in the One Word, her Only-begotten Son, to those who are far off and peace to those who are near, since through herself, in the second place we all have access in the one Spirit to the Father (Eph. 2, 14-17)." For she crushed the head of the serpent.[11]

The Italian Archbishop, Ambrose Catarino († 1553) continues the Dominican reflection on Coredemption by teaching that both Christ and his Mother merited our Redemption through their joint sufferings: "This generation is from both — that is, from a Man and a woman, from Christ and Mary; because both, although they were completely innocent (Mary was such through Christ), nevertheless . . . merited salvation for us by their sufferings — first indeed and principally Christ as Man, and then the Virgin herself as woman."[12]

Catarino also cites the New Eve model in defense of the key distinction between the sufficiency of Christ's Redemption and the fittingness of Mary's association with Jesus as his helpmate:

> The glorious work of the Redemption for which she was chosen proves clearly that it

> was fitting that in some way she be an associate of Christ — not that Christ Himself did not suffice, but because it was good and fitting that He have a helpmate Himself. For just as from a woman came the beginning of death . . . so also from a woman had to come the beginning of life. For this is the most common opinion of the ancients.[13]

When one of the foremost theologians of the Council of Trent becomes the champion of Mary Co-redemptrix, the theological and doctrinal credibility of the Co-redemption title becomes promulgated throughout Catholic theological circles. Jesuit Father Alphonsus Salmerón († 1585), renowned theologian, exegete, and one of the original followers of St. Ignatius, repeatedly explains and defends the title of Co-redemptrix in an unprecedented systematic treatment of the doctrine.

In a remarkable passage, Salmerón defends the Marian titles of Co-redemptrix, Mediatrix, Advocate, and others as legitimate titles which rightly bespeak of the goodness and glory of Mary, full of grace:

> Truly Mary, very near and uniquely joined to Him, is called full of grace . . . how much He prepared that she as mother would pour out the fullest graces among us all as her sons as one who had been assumed by

> Christ, not out of any necessity, or out of weakness, but on account of the necessity to share and make clear, certainly, the goodness and glory in the mother that she would be (if it is permitted thus to speak) co-redemptrix, mediatrix, cooperatrix of the salvation of mankind and to whom, as to an individual advocate, all the faithful ought to approach and fly for help.[14]

It is appropriate that the doctrinal maturity of Co-redemptrix generally takes place side by side with the development of the doctrine of the Immaculate Conception (which led to the latter's solemn papal definition in 1854).

Once again we must affirm that Mary is Co-redemptrix only because she was first the Immaculate Conception. God the Father prepares her for this great battle for souls through her total enmity against the Evil One. The pure, perfect Virgin partakes in the greatest of all sacrifices, so that grace can flow to humanity through the same immaculate channel from which Christ the First Grace passes into humanity. Grace is thereupon distributed to the human family free from the limitations of a channel tainted by sin, so as to allow its greatest possible efficacy in the human heart who receives it. Later popes will confirm that the mystery of her Coredemption cannot be understood outside of an understanding of her fullness of grace.[15]

Salmerón goes on to note that the participation of Mary Co-redemptrix does not distract, but rather adds glory to Christ himself, for all her excellence and her capacity to share in redeeming is derived from the redeeming capacity of Jesus:

> The Mother stood near the Cross for this: that the restoration of mankind would correspond with the collapse of the world. As the fall of the world was accomplished by two, but especially by a man, so the salvation and redemption came about from two, but especially from Christ; for whatever excellence Mary has, she received from Christ, not only on account of a certain proper harmony, but also on account of the eminent capacity of Christ in redeeming, a capacity which with his mother (whose works He needed least of all) He wished to share as co-redemptrix, not only without her dishonor, but with the great glory of Christ Himself.[16]

According to Salmerón, the simple motive of the Co-redemptrix in the exercise of her many functions on behalf of humanity, which are identified in her titles, is Christian maternal love: "For love of us . . . she is all ours who is called Mother of Mercy, Queen of heaven, Mistress of the world, Star of the sea, advocate, co-redemptrix, preserver, mother of God."[17]

Throughout Salmerón's extraordinary treatment on Marian Coredemption we find the repeated use of the prefix, "co," in emphasizing the Mother's rightful subordination and dependency on the Lord of Redemption. He refers to the Mother's "co-suffering,"[18] "co-misery,"[19] "co-sorrowing"[20]; that she was "co-crucified,"[21] that she "co-died,"[22] "co-suffered," "co-operated,"[23] and was "co-united"[24] with Jesus in the Redemption. This clear and generous theology of Mary Co-redemptrix provides solid dogmatic foundation for the following century's explosion of theological literature on Coredemption.

We conclude the sixteenth century with the Marian teachings of another Jesuit and Doctor of the Church, St. Peter Canisius († 1597). The Dutch-born theologian and "Second Apostle of Germany" speaks of the Mother's redemptive offering of her Son-Victim at Calvary: "Standing under the cross of her Son, she remained intrepid in her faith, and offered Christ, a true and living Victim, for the expiation of the sins of the world."[25]

Notes

[1] *Orat. ms S. Petri Slaisburgens., saec.* XV; Codex Petrin. a, III, 20 and *Orat. ms S. Petri saec.* XIV, XV; Codex Petrin. a, I, 20, quoted by G. M. DREVES, *Analecta hymnica medii aevi,* Leipzig, Reisland, t. 46, 1905, p. 126, n. 79. The original Latin is as follows:

20. *Pia dulcis et benigna*
Nullo prorsus luctu digna
Si fletum hinc eligeres
Ut compassa redemptori
Captivato transgressori
Tu corredemptrix *fieres*

21. *Tunc non tantum condolere*
Moestae matri se debere
Me cerno grates solvere
Tibi meae redemptrici
Quae de manu inimici
Dignatur me evolvere

[2] St. Bernard was most likely the first to use the term "compassion"; *PL* 183, 438A; cf. R. Laurentin, *Le Titre de Corédemptrice*, p. 15.

[3] Arnold of Chartres wrote that Mary co-operated abundantly and exceedingly in our Redemption and was "co-crucified" and "co-died" with her Son; cf. *Tractatus de septem verbis Domini in cruce*; tr. 3; *PL* 189, 1694, 1695 A, 1693 B.

[4] Pseudo-Albert, *Mariale*, q. 42, 4; q. 29, 3; q. 150.

[5] For example, cf. J. B. Petitlot, *Coronula mariana,* Molinis, Fudez, 1866, c. 4, art. 2, I, p. 248; S. M. Giraud, S.M., *Prêtre et hostie*, Lyon, Delhomme, 1885, Conclusion, 5, t. II, p. 577.

[6] St. Antoninus, *Summa Theologica*, pars 4, tit. 15, cap. 20, paragr. 14; ed. Veronae, 1740, col. 1064.

[7] *Ibid.*, c. 44, art. 3; ed. Veronae, t. 4, 1254 E.

[8] Cf. F. Godts, *De Definibilitate Mediationis Universalis Deiparae*, Bruxellis, 1904, p. 212.

[9] St. Antoninus, *Summa Theologica*, pars 4, tit. 15, cap. 14, paragr. 2; ed. Veronae, col. 1002.

[10] Cf. Chapter XI; For papal reference to Mediatrix of all graces inclusive of John Paul II, cf. Chapter IV, note 11.

[11] Work without title; incipit: *In hoc opere contenta. In Cant. cant.*

homiliae quindecim. In aliq. Ps. . . . In supersanctam Dei genitricem Mariam panegyrici . . . P. H, Stephanus, 1515. *Sermo 4 in Deigenitr.*, fol. 207 r.; reedited in Alva y Astorga, P., *Bibliotheca Virg.*, Madrid, 1648, III, 525 BC 2.

[12] A. Catarino, O.P., *De Immaculata Conceptione Virginis Mariae opusculum*, disp. Lib. 3, persuasio 14; ed. Alva y Astorga, *Bibliotheca virginalis Mariae* . . . , Matriti, 1648, vol. 2, p. 56.

[13] *Ibid.*, Lib. 3, persuasio 5; ed. Alva y Astorga, vol. 2, p. 47.

[14] Alphonsus Salmerón, *Commentarii in Evangel.*, Tr. 5, Opera, Cologne, ed., Hiérat, 1604, t. III, pp. 37b- 38a;

[15] Cf. John Paul II, *L'Osservatore Romano*, English edition, December 12, 1983, p. 1.

[16] Salmerón, *Commentarii*, vol. 10, tr. 41, p. 359b.

[17] *Ibid.*, vol. 11, tr. 38, p. 312a.

[18] *Ibid.*, vol. 3, tr. 43, 495a; cf. X, 51, 425 a; cf. Laurentin, *Le Titre de Corédemptrice*, pp. 15-16.

[19] *Ibid.*, vol. 3, 51, 426a, 424a, 429 b; vol. 11, 38, 311b; vol. 10, 51, 426a; cf. Laurentin, *Le Titre de Corédemptrice*, pp. 15-16.

[20] *Ibid.*, vol. 3, 43, 495a.

[21] *Ibid.*, vol. 3, 43, 399 b; vol. 11, 2, 188a.

[22] *Ibid.*, vol. 10, 51, 426b.

[23] *Ibid.*, vol. 6, 6, 39a.

[24] *Ibid.*, 36b.

[25] St. Peter Canisius, *De Maria Incomparabili Virgine*, 1. 4. c. 26; cf. Bourassé, *Summa Aurea de Laudibus B. M. Virginis*, vol. 8, col. 1425.

Chapter IX

The Golden Age of Mary Co-redemptrix

The extraordinary testimonies to Mary Co-redemptrix previously offered by the likes of St. Bernard, Arnold of Chartres, Pseudo-Albert, John Tauler, and Alphonsus Salmerón became the ordinary and "common opinion of theologians"[1] in the seventeenth century, which can legitimately be referred to as the "Golden Age of Marian Coredemption."

In the 1600's alone, references to the Immaculate Mother's unique and active participation "with Jesus" in the Redemption number well over three hundred. Within these references are numerous explanations and defenses of the titles of Redemptrix and Co-redemptrix, coupled with learned theological defenses of the sound doctrine which the titles convey.[2]

So generous and penetrating is the theological treatment of the Mother Co-redemptrix throughout this Golden Age that its contribution lays the theological foundation for the systematic treatment of the doctrine in later centuries. Under the classic categories of Christian soteriology (theology of salvation) in which Our Lord's Redemption is considered, that is, merit, satisfaction, sacrifice, and redemptive ransom, the Mother's Coredemption is fundamentally treated under these categories by the theological minds and hearts of this age.[3] So many in number were they, we can offer only a sampling of the theological laud and love to Mary Co-redemptrix that this era provides.[4]

Of utmost importance to the story of Mary Co-redemptrix is its organic progression through this critical phrase of the Church's theological history, for the doctrine of Coredemption and its "theological foundations" are firmly embedded in Tradition, and will, in future centuries, receive their magisterial sanctions directly from the popes.

St. Lawrence of Brindisi († 1619), Franciscan Doctor of the Church, uses the concept of Mary's "spiritual priesthood" (in a mode analogous to the priesthood of the laity as discussed at the Second Vatican Council)[5] to illustrate Mary's participation in the Redemption in the category of sacrifice. Sacrifice soteriologically refers to Christ's free immolation and offering of himself to the Eternal Father in a truly priestly action for humanity's sins. Mary in her "spiritual priesthood," as St. Lawrence explains, shares in the offering of the one redemptive sacrifice at Calvary with Jesus, the "Principal Priest":

> Did not Mary put her life in danger for us, when she stood by the cross of Christ truly sacrificing Him to God in spirit, as full, abundantly full of the spirit of Abraham, and offering Him in true charity for the

> salvation of the world? . . . The spirit of Mary was a spiritual priest, as the cross was the altar and Christ the sacrifice; although the spirit of Christ was the principal priest, the spirit of Mary was there together with the spirit of Christ; indeed it was one spirit with Him as one soul in two bodies. Hence the spirit of Mary together with the spirit of Christ performed the priestly office at the altar of the cross and offered the sacrifice of the cross for the salvation of the world to the Eternal God . . . . For of her, as of God to Whom she was most similar in spirit, we can truly say that she so loved the world as to give her only-begotten Son so that everyone who believes in Him will not perish, but will have life eternal.[6]

Mary is not a "priest" in the formal sense, since she is not ordained, and therefore cannot offer a formal sacrifice. Rather, she possesses a spiritual priesthood true of all the baptized, but in the highest possible degree due to her singular dignity. In view of her fullness of grace and her coredemptive mission with the Redeemer, it is clear that her spiritual sacrifice in subordinate participation "with Jesus" the High Priest, exceeds in spiritual fruitfulness the sacrifice of any ministerial priest, excepting only her own Son.[7]

Another Doctor of the Church and revered

counter-reformational cardinal and theologian, St. Robert Bellarmine († 1621), teaches the uniqueness of the Mother's co-operation in his metaphor of spiritual creation:

> Even if Mary was not present at the creation of the material heavens, nevertheless she was present at the creation of the spiritual heavens — the Apostles; and although she was not present at the founding of the material earth, nevertheless she was present at the founding of the spiritual earth — the Church. For she alone co-operated in the mystery of the Incarnation; she alone co-operated in the mystery of the Passion, standing before the cross, and offering her Son for the salvation of the world.[8]

The Jesuit theologian, de Salazar († 1646) puts forward a theological defense of the Immaculate Virgin's direct, immediate, and formal cooperation in Redemption.[9] De Salazar justifies the titles of Redemptrix, Reparatrix, and Mediatrix among others, and in a later work refers to the Mother as the "Co-redemptrix."[10]

The theological concept of "ransom" refers to the "payment of a price," and the price of Redemption is precisely the merits and satisfactions of the Redeemer offered to the Eternal Father for our salvation, freeing us from Satan's bondage. To what degree, then, does the Mother participate in the ransom of "buying back" the human race together with Christ?

The testimony of this Golden Age gives witness to two ways in which the Immaculate One participates in the ransom obtained by her Son: firstly, that Mary paid the same price (although subordinately) which her Son paid in offering the merits and satisfaction of her Son to the Eternal Father; secondly, that Mary offered her own merits and satisfactions in union with her Son's for man's Redemption.

The French author, Fr. Raphael of the Discalced Augustinians († 1639), illustrates the Mother's subordinate "servant" role in the buying back of humanity as Co-redemptrix:

> Her Son shares with her and conveys to her in some way the glory of our ransom, an act which she truly did not perform, nor was able to carry out in order to satisfy the Father by the rigor of justice . . . But we can say that she cooperated in our ransom in that she gave the Redeemer flesh and blood, substance and price of our ransom. She did so just as a servant cooperated in the buying back of a slave if she lent the money to her master for the deliverance. Also, she cooperated because she willingly consented to see Him die and she generously condemned herself to the same torture . . . which rightly gives her

> the quality of coredemptrix of man although her Son is the principal and formal cause of our salvation.[11]

The Franciscan Mariologist, Angelo Vulpes († 1647), explains the capacity of the Co-redemptrix to pay the "death-debt" of sinners: "Mary died in imitation of her Son in order that she, in her capacity as Co-redemptrix, might with full merit pay the death-debt of others."[12] In addition, Vulpes points out that it was God's decree that man would be redeemed by the "united merits" of Jesus and Mary: "God decreed to redeem all men from the servitude of sin . . . through their merits [i.e., the merits of Christ and Mary] . . . He decreed the passibility of the future Christ, and likewise that of His Mother, so that she too might become the Co-redemptrix of the entire human race."[13]

The Merits of Christ and Mary

How do we understand the Catholic concept of supernatural merit, and in what dimension of this can humanity participate? Jesus Christ, through his passion and death, merited "reward" for humanity, namely our justification.[14] But human creatures may also "merit" in the sense that God has placed a supernatural value on certain human acts, and if freely performed by man, God rewards his sons and daughters with an increase of his grace and divine goodness for themselves and for others.[15] How, then, does the Immaculate Mother uniquely share in the merits of Christ for the Redemption of the world?

During this period, the specific nature of Our Lady's merits is theologically discussed[16] for the first time since its introduction by Eadmer of Canterbury. The Spaniard, P. M. Frangipane († 1638), identifies the object of merit for the Immaculate Co-redemptrix as the same as that merited by Christ, but on the substantially different level of "*de congruo*" or "fittingness" compared to the "*de condigno*" level of "justice" merited by the divine Redeemer alone: ". . . Everything which Christ merited for us *de condigno* was merited for us *de congruo* by Mary . . . . This title, Co-redemptrix requires innocence on her part; for how could she cleanse the world from sin, if she herself were subject to sin?"[17]

The thesis that Mary merited for us *de congruo* that which Jesus merited for us *de condigno* became a common teaching of the period and was later given papal approval by St. Pius X.[18] In essence, Mary merited in the order of fittingness that which Jesus merited in the order of justice and equality between himself and the Father.[19]

The same notion of Our Lady's merit is repeated by numerous authors during the century, for example by the Jesuit, George de Rhodes († 1661):

> We must state first of all that Mary can be called Redemptrix of mankind in a certain true and proper sense, although not as primary and proper as Christ . . . . Mary

> merited *de congruo* through her co-passion and prayers everything which Christ merited for us *de condigno* through His death . . . She merited, first of all, that we should be liberated from all sin, both original and personal, that is, all graces which precede and cause our justification . . . .[20]

The Franciscan Roderick de Portillo, O.F.M. (c. 1630), also confirms that Jesus and Mary obtained the same object of merit for humanity, albeit in their respective degrees: "There is no doubt that the Blessed Virgin [at Calvary] merited the same thing which her Son merited."[21] The contemplative author, Novati († 1648), affirms the unified meritorious offering of Jesus and Mary for human Redemption: "Just as Christ *de condigno* merited sufficiently for all men the remission of sins, sanctifying grace and all the other goods that follow from it . . . so it must be said that the Blessed Virgin *de congruo* merited the same things for all men."[22] In addition, Novati re-affirms: "I say first that the Virgin, by co-suffering with Christ, did co-operate in human Redemption. I say secondly that she most greatly co-operated in the Redemption of the human race by offering the life and blood of her Son to the Eternal Father for men's salvation . . . . The will of Christ and Mary was one, and there was one holocaust." [23]

The saving action of the Redeemer results in a suprabundant compensation for the sins of humanity. This compensation constitutes the theological concept of "satisfaction," the appeasing of the guilt of humanity's sin whereby the justice of God is satisfied, which results in the restoration of the saving communion between man and God. In this, too, the Mother shares, and thus the seventeenth century theologians voice their assent to the satisfactory participation of the Co-redemptrix. Numerous authors speak of Mary's satisfaction in a *de congruo* degree at Calvary, in a manner similar though distinct from her meritorious participation.[24]

With the prophetic revelations of Venerable Mary of Agreda († 1665) contained in the *Mystical City of God*, Christian mysticism once again assists the development of the Co-redemptrix story. In this prophetic work, the Spanish mystic calls Our Lady the "Redemptrix" and speaks of her consequential role of distributing the fruits of Redemption in light of her primary role as a participant in the Redemption:

> Just as she cooperated with the passion and gave her Son to take part in the human lineage, so the same Lord made her participant of the dignity of Redemptrix, having given her the merits and the fruits of Redemption so that she can distribute them and with one hand communicate all this to those redeemed.[25]

In the later part of the century, a tract against the Co-redemptrix title and doctrine was penned by the

German author, Adam Widenfeld, and received significant distribution.[26] But within two years, approximately forty theological defenses were written to counter Widenfeld's objection to calling Mary the "Co-redemptrix."[27] One excellent example is the response of the Prague professor, Maximillian Reichenberger (c. 1677), who vindicates the role and the merits of Mary Co-redemptrix in context of the New Eve model:

> We most freely admit that Christ did not need the help of His Mother in redeeming the human race; but we deny that the merits and prayers of His Mother were not joined, *per modum meriti de congruo,* with the merits *de condigno* of her Son. It is evident that the Fathers could term the Blessed Virgin Coredemptrix of the human race with much more reason than they could term Eve . . . the cause of our ruin . . . . For Eve co-operated in our ruin only remotely and accidentally . . . . while Mary co-operated in the Redemption of the human race *proximately and immediately*, not only communicating to Christ the price of our Redemption from her own blood, but also aiding Him and assisting Him, and suffering with Him up to the consummation of the redemptive work on the cross.[28]

The tract of Widenfeld attacking Co-redemptrix was later placed on the *Index of Forbidden Books* by the Holy See.[29]

Unambiguous in its theological praises and defenses of the Immaculate Co-redemptrix, the seventeenth century Golden Age provides dogmatic foundations for future centuries to penetrate more deeply the mystery of the Woman at Calvary with theological precision and with heartfelt piety. The providential combination of theology and devotion, of "head and heart," dedicated to the coredemptive Mother during this century, is perhaps best represented in a theological meditation by the Doctor of the Church and great apostle of the Hearts of Jesus and Mary,[30] St. John Eudes († 1680), who quotes the Fathers and the mystics in his theological laud of the "Co-redemptrix with Christ":

> The salvation of immortal souls is also the great work of the Mother of God. Why did Almighty God choose the Blessed Virgin Mary to be the Mother of God? Why did He preserve her from original sin and make her holy from the very first moment of her life? Why did He shower upon her so many privileges, ornamenting her with grace and virtue? Why did He confer upon her so much wisdom, goodness, meekness and such great power in heaven, hell, and on earth? It was simply

that she might be worthy to cooperate with her Divine Son in man's redemption. All the Fathers of the Church say clearly that she is Co-redemptrix with Christ in the work of our salvation. I hear Our Lord and His Blessed Mother saying to St. Bridget, whose revelations are approved by the Church, that Adam and Eve lost the world by eating an apple, but that they saved it by a heart: *quasi uno Corde mundum salvavimus* (*Revel. Extravag.* Cap. 3), that is Our Lord and His Mother had but one heart, one love, one sentiment, one mind and one will with each other. As the Sacred Heart of Jesus was a furnace of love for men, so the heart of His loving Mother was inflamed with charity and zeal for souls. Christ immolated Himself upon the cross for the redemption of mankind and Mary made a similar sacrifice in undergoing untold sufferings and sorrows.[31]

Notes

[1] F. de Guerra, O.F.M., *Majestas gratiarum ac virtutum omnium Deiparae Virginis Mariae*, vol. 2, Hispali, 1659, lib. 3, disc. 4, fragm. 10, n. 36.

[2] Cf. Carol, *De Corredemptione*, pp. 198–480. According to the valuable (though limited) study by Laurentin, from the seventeenth to the nineteenth century the term Redemptrix was gradually replaced with that of Co-redemptrix. Before the seventeenth century Redemptrix is used by ten authors and Co-redemptrix by three authors. During the seventeenth century Redemptrix is still preferred fifty-one times to Co-redemptrix's twenty-seven times. By the eighteenth century, Co-redemptrix is being used more than Redemptrix by a twenty-four to sixteen margin, and by the nineteenth century Redemptrix virtually disappears, with some exceptions. Cf. R. Laurentin, *Le Titre de Corédemptrice*, p. 19.

Note: Along with these valuable statistics, Laurentin offers some strong conclusions of his own regarding the titles of Redemptrix and Co-redemptrix, which do not appear substantiated by his and other sources. For example, the author states: "But when in the twelfth century, the passage from *causa causae* (Mary, cause of the Redeemer) developed into the expression of *causa causati* (cause of Redemption), . . . the term Redemptrix could not without serious ambiguity translate these realities." But the concept of Mary's participation in the Redemption as a sharing in the "*causa causati*" in reference to Redemption was intrinsic to the most ancient testimonies of the New Eve as the woman who played an active and instrumental role in salvation, and was gradually brought to its natural development in the explicit teachings of Mary's active role in Redemption at Calvary as articulated by St. Bernard, Arnold of Chartres, St. Albert, and John Tauler.

Moreover, the title Redemptrix was used in the Church in an orthodox and balanced manner for five centuries after the twelfth century, and without any "serious ambiguity," but precisely the same way "Mediatrix" is used in relation to "Mediator" today –

subordinate, dependent, and totally relying upon the primacy of the divine Redeemer. That Co-redemptrix as a title eventually phased out the use of Redemptrix can be seen as a positive development without casting dispersion on the legitimacy of Redemptrix, which was used in the Church for over seven hundred years in a balanced fashion by doctors, theologians, mystics, and saints.

The author goes on to refer to the titles of Redemptrix and Co-redemptrix as "somewhat disturbing" during this time of historical development, and concludes: "we have the impression that co-redemptrix and, even more so, redemptrix, have slowed down the development of the following thesis of Mary's cooperation in Redemption." In fact, the historical evidence appears to support the opposite conclusion, that the terms in fact have assisted in the process of the historical development of doctrine. The greater frequency of both terms from the twelfth century to the eighteenth centuries parallels the time of greatest theological development of the doctrine of Mary's cooperation in Redemption, as is particularly the case in the seventeenth century Golden Age, during which the terms are used in greatest quantity and the theology of the role receives its greatest historical treatment.

Moreover, the terms Co-redemptrix and Redemptrix truly capture the full meaning of the doctrine of Mary's unique participation with the Redeemer in the historic victory over Satan and sin. Rather than some minimalized or vague concept of the doctrine, the Co-redemptrix title envelops the full dynamism of the role of being Christ's unique partner in Redemption, and therefore contributed to an honest discussion of its intrinsic meaning and development. This remains true whether one be "pro" or "con" to the Coredemption doctrine, and hence the Co-redemptrix title has historically served, and continues to serve, as an authentic component of the doctrinal development of Mary's cooperation in Redemption.

[3] For extended treatments of Coredemption under the same four classic soteriological categories, cf. Gregory Alastruey, *The Blessed*

Virgin Mary, English translation of the original by Sr. M. J. La Giglia, O.P., Herder, 1964, ch. 2; Friethoff, O.P., *A Complete Mariology*, Blackfriars, 1958, English translation of Dutch original, Part III, ch. I-V; specifically during this seventeenth century period in its four traditional categories; J. B. Carol, "Our Lady's Coredemption," *Mariology* vol. 2, Bruce, 1957, pp. 400-409.

[4] For a fuller explanation of the seventeenth century references to Coredemption, cf. Carol, *De Corredemptione*, pp. 198-480.

[5] Cf. *Lumen Gentium*, 10; cf. 1. Pet. 2:9-10.

[6] St. Lawrence of Brindisi, *Mariale*; *Opera Omnia*, Patavii, 1928, vol. 1, pp. 183-184.

[7] Cf. Carol, "Our Lady's Coredemption," vol. 2, p. 418; M. O'Carroll, C.S.Sp., *Theotokos: A Theological Encyclopedia of the Blessed Virgin Mary*, Michael Glazier, 1982, pp. 293-296.

[8] St. Robert Bellarmine, *Cod. Vat. Lat. Ottob.* 2424, f. 193, cited by C. Dillenschneider, *Marie au service de notre Rédemption*, p. 208. Bellarmine's contemporary and brother Jesuit, Suarez († 1617), known as the Father of Modern systematic Mariology, also contributes to the Coredemption discussion in *De Incarn.*, disp. 23.

[9] F. Chirino de Salazar, S.J., *In Proverbiis,* VIII, 19, n. 222, Cologne ed., ap. J. Kinchium, 1621, t. I, 627; for another use of Redemptrix by Salazar, cf. *Pro Immaculata conceptione defensio*, Compluti, of J. Gratiani, 1618, CXXI, § I, pp. 132 b-133 a.

[10] Cf. de Salazar, *In Canticum*, Lyon, Prost, 1643, t. 1, p. 128.

[11] Father Raphael, *Les sacrifices de la Vierge et de la France*, speech given in Aix, February 2, 1639, 2nd ed. Avignon, I. Piot [s.d.], pp. 32-34.

[12] A. Vulpes, *Sacrae Theologiae Summa Joannis D. Scoti, Doctoris Subtilissimus, et Commentaria*, Neapoli, 1646, vol. 3, pars 4, pp. 498-499.

[13] *Ibid.*, pp. 290-291.

[14] Cf. Council of Trent, D 799.

[15] Cf. Council of Trent (1547): DS 1546; 1548; *Catechism of the Catholic Church*, Part 3, ch. 3, art. 2, sec. 3, nn. 2006-2011.

[16] Perhaps the first author treating Mary's *de congruo* merit is de

Salazar; cf. Carol, "Our Lady's Coredemption," p. 401, note 94.

[17] P. M. Frangipane, *Blasones de la Virgen Madre de Dios y Señora nuestra*, Zaragoza, 1635, pp. 65-66.

[18] St. Pius X, *Ad Diem Illum*; *ASS* 36, p. 453; The magisterial statement by Pope St. Pius X regarding Mary's merit *de congruo* should serve as an authoritative *aurea media in veritate* (golden mean in truth) in the debates over the nature and degree of Mary's merit as Co-redemptrix. Without saying the last word on whether or not Mary also merited *de digno, de supercongruo*, or *de condigno ex mera condignitate* (just as the dogma of the Assumption did not say the last word concerning the debate over the "Death" of Mary), St. Pius X's statement should serve as an authoritative confirmation that Mary *at least* merited *de congruo* as Christ merited *de condigno*, and as such should serve as a consensus doctrinal statement regarding the question of Mary's coredemptive merit.

[19] Cf. Chapter XI for a further discussion of the nature and levels of supernatural merit and its relation to the Blessed Virgin.

[20] G. de Rhodes, S.J., *Disputationes Theologicae Scholasticae*, Lugduni, 1676, vol. 2, tract. 8: *De Deipara Virgine Maria*, disp. Unica, quaest. 5, sect. 3, p. 265.

[21] R. de Portillo, O.F.M., *Libro de los tratados de Cristo Señor nuestro, y de su santísima Madre, y de los beneficios y Mercedes que goza el mundo por su medio*, Tauri, 1630, p. 41.

[22] J. Novati, *De Eminentia Deiparae*, Bononiae, 1639, vol. 2, p. 236.

[23] *Ibid.*, vol. 1, ch. 18, q. 14, p. 379-380.

[24] Cf. Carol, "Our Lady's Coredemption," p. 403; cf. D. González Matheo, O.F.M., *Mystica Civitas Dei vindicata . . .* , Matriti, 1747, p. 124, nn. 368-371; cf. A. Peralta, S.J., *Dissertationes Scholasticae de Sacratissima Virgine Maria*, Mexici, 1726, p. 264; cf. Th. de Almeyda, *La compassion aux douleurs de Marie*, ed. Braine-le-Compte, 1902, pp. 161-163; cf. G. Federici, O.S.B., *Tractatus polemicus de Matre Dei*, vol. 1, Neapoli, 1777, p. 106; cf. G. A. Nasi, *Le grandezze di Maria Vergine . . .* , Venezia, 1717, p. 197.

[25] Ven. Mary of Agreda, *Mystical City of God*, ed. Amberes, H. and C. Verdussen, 1696, P. I, L. I, c. 18, n. 274, p. 86b.

[26] A. von Widenfeld, *Monita salutaria Beatae Virginis Mariae . . .*, Ghent, 1673, moniyum 10.

[27] Cf. Carol, *De Corredemptione*, pp. 302-318.

[28] M. Reichenberger, *Mariani cultus vindiciae, sive nonnullae animadversions in libellum cui titulus: Monita Salutaria B . V. Mariae ad cultures suos indiscretos, pro vindicanda contra auctorem anonymum Deiparae Gloria, secundum orthodoxae fidei dogmata, Sanctorum Patrum testimonia, rectae rationis dictamina et theologorum principia*, Pragae, 1677, p. 120.

[29] Pope Alexander VIII condemned the phrase: "the praise which is given to Mary qua Maria is vain"; DH 2326; cf. A. M. Calero, *La Vergine Maria nel mistero di Cristo e della Chiesa. Saggio di mariologia*, Turin, 1995, p. 284.

[30] Cf. Pius XI, *Decree of Canonization* of Bl. John Eudes, May 31, 1925.

[31] St. John Eudes, *The Priest, His Dignity and Obligations*, P. J, Kenedy & Sons, 1947, pp. 134-135. This quoted passage was originally published in a work entitled, *The Good Confessor* in 1666.

Chapter X

"There Is No Other Single Word"

The Mariological fruits of the Golden Age sustain Marian thought on Coredemption for two successive centuries. The eighteenth and nineteenth centuries do not bring forth any substantially new harvest of insight into the Mother Co-redemptrix, but did witness a much more generous use of the title of Co-redemptrix in the fields of both theology and spirituality. By the end of the nineteenth century, "Co-redemptrix" clearly becomes the dominant title to convey the Mother of God's saving collaboration in Redemption, and is used in hundreds of testimonies by a plethora of theologians, saints, and mystics.[1] The Redemptrix title, on the other hand, essentially falls out of common usage during this period.

The Marian master, St. Louis Grignion de Montfort († 1716) from whom John Paul II derives his Marian motto of consecration, "Totus Tuus" ("entirely yours"), preaches that the coredemptive sacrifice of the Mother throughout her life is a glorification of our Lord's own independence precisely through "depending" on the Virgin Mother:

> . . . [Our Blessed Lord] glorified His

> independence and His majesty in depending on that sweet Virgin, in His conception, in His birth, in His presentation in the temple, in His hidden life of thirty years, and even in His death where she was to be present in order that He might make with her but one same sacrifice, and be immolated to the Eternal Father by her consent, just as Isaac of old was offered by Abraham's consent to the will of God. It is she who nourished Him, supported Him, brought Him up, and then sacrificed Him for us.[2]

The Franciscan author, Charles del Moral († 1731) may be the first theologian to teach that the merits of the Immaculate Co-redemptrix, while being totally dependent upon the merits of Jesus, were also in themselves "condign" merits in a secondary sense. Our Lady's merits, according to del Moral, were more than just "fitting" or congruous (*de congruo*) but also worthy, not in strict justice, but in relation to and dependency upon the superabundant merits of the Redeemer:

> The Mother of God at the foot of the cross, co-suffering and offering her Son to the Eternal Father, with her Son and by her merits satisfied in a sense (*secundum quid*), but *de condigno* and only secondarily, as the

> Co-redemptrix, for the sins of the whole human race.[3]

And further:

> . . . the Mother of God co-operated with her Son in the salvation of men, the grace and glory of the angels, by acts meritorious *de condigno*, but dependent on the merits of her Son. Therefore, in that sense we say that it now seems consistent with theological principles that whatever Christ the Lord merited for us falls also under the condign — and not merely the congruous — merits of the Mother of God, dependent . . . on the superabundant merits of her Son.[4]

Marian Doctor of the Church and Redemptorist founder, St. Alphonsus de Liguori († 1787), invokes the Madonna of Calvary under the "Redemptrix" title, in acknowledgement of the merits of her sacrifice at Calvary: "By the great merit that she acquired in this great sacrifice, she is called redemptrix."[5] The Doctor of Mary's Universal Mediation also calls her the "Co-redemptrix,"[6] and explains how her Coredemption at Calvary is the means by which she becomes the spiritual "Mother of our souls":

> "She offered to the Eternal Father with so much grief in her own heart, the life of

> her beloved Son for our salvation. Hence St. Augustine testifies that, having co-operated by her love in order that the faithful be born to the life of grace, by that she became spiritual Mother of all who are members of our head Jesus Christ."[7]

> And:

> Christ provided that the Blessed Virgin, through the sacrifice and oblation of His life, co-operate in our salvation and thus become the Mother of our souls. And our Savior wished to signify this when, before He died, looking down from the cross at His Mother and disciple standing there, He first said to Mary: "Behold thy Son" — as if to say: "Behold, now man is born to the life of grace on account of the oblation of My life made by you for his salvation."[8]

As to the unity of will and singularity of sacrifice offered by Jesus and Mary, St. Alphonsus expounds:

> In the death of Jesus, Mary united her will to that of her Son, in such a way that both offered one and the same Sacrifice; and therefore the holy Abbot [Arnold of Chartres] says that thus the Son and the

> Mother accomplished the Redemption of the human race, obtaining salvation for men —Jesus by satisfying for our sins, and Mary by obtaining for us that this satisfaction be applied to us.[9]

Venerable John Henry Newman and Fr. Fredrick William Faber

By the middle of the nineteenth century, we have the corroboration of Venerable Cardinal John Henry Newman († 1890), one of the most quoted theological sources at the Second Vatican Council. Newman defends Mary Co-redemptrix in his dialogue with the Anglican clergyman Pusey by reason of the title's relation to the other glorious patristic titles granted to Christ's Mother: "When they found you with the Fathers calling her Mother of God, Second Eve, and Mother of all Living, the Mother of Life, the Morning Star, the Mystical New Heaven, the Sceptre of Orthodoxy, the All-undefiled Mother of Holiness, and the like, they would have deemed it a poor compensation for such language, that you protested against her being called a Co-redemptrix . . . ."[10]

A valuable apologetic contribution to the legitimate usage of Co-redemptrix comes from the pen of Newman's colleague in the Oxford movement, the founder of the London Oratory, Fr. Fredrick William Faber († 1863). Though more disposed to the popular heart than to the speculative mind, Faber's commentary on the title provides several important distinctions which benefit a precise concept and pastoral use of Mary Co-redemptrix for the common faithful.[11]

Faber begins with an honest overview of the Co-redemptrix title in light of the testimonies of saints and doctors, yet bears in mind the need to protect the uniqueness of Christ as sole divine Redeemer:

> Saints and doctors have united in calling our Blessed Lady co-redemptrix (co-redemptress) of the world. There is no question of the lawfulness of using such language, because there is such overwhelming authority for it. The question is as to its meaning. Is it merely the hyperbole of panegyric, the affectionate exaggeration of devotion, the inevitable language of a true understanding of Mary, which finds common language inadequate to convey the whole truth? Or is it literally true, with an acknowledged and recognized theological accuracy attached to it? This is a question which has presented itself to most minds in connection with devotion to our Blessed Mother, and there are few questions to which more vague and unsatisfactory answers have been made, than to this. On the one hand, it seems rash to assert of language used both by

> saints and doctors, that it is only exaggeration and hyperbole, flowery phraseology intended to startle, but without any real meaning hidden beneath it. On the other hand, who can doubt that our most Blessed Lord is the sole Redeemer of the world, His Precious Blood the sole ransom from sin, and that Mary herself, though in a different way, needed redemption as much as we do, and received it in a more copious manner and after a more magnificent kind in the mystery of the Immaculate Conception?[12]

Faber condemns a false concept of "redemptrix" which would erroneously designate Mary as a female redeemer parallel to Christ. But he also applauds the accurate sense of the doctrine particularly conveyed in the compound term, Co-redemptrix: "We certainly shrink from asserting that the language of the saints has no meaning, or is inadvisable; and, at the same time, we have no doubt that our Blessed Lady is not the co-redemptrix of the world in the strict sense of being redemptrix, in the unshared sense in which our Lord is Redeemer of the world, but she is co-redemptrix in the accurate sense of that compound word."[13]

Faber describes how all the Christian baptized are called to participate in an analogous way in the work of Redemption in the application of redemptive graces to souls, commenting upon St. Paul's co-suffering call of Colossians 1:24 (the same call which will later be exhorted by twentieth century popes to become "co-redeemers"[14]):

> The elect co-operate with [Christ] in this work as His members. They have become His members by redeeming grace, that is, by the application to their souls of His sole redemption. By His merits they have acquired the ability of meriting. Their works can satisfy for sin, the sins of others as well as their own, by their union with Him. Thus, to use St. Paul's language, by their sanctified sufferings or by their voluntary penances they "fill up in the bodies that which is lacking of the sufferings of Christ, for His Body's sake, which is the Church." Thus by the communion of the saints in their Head, Jesus Christ, the work of redemption is perpetually going on by the accomplishment and application of the redemption effected on the Cross by our Blessed Lord. It is not a figurative and symbolical, but a real and substantial, co-operation of the elect with our Blessed Redeemer. There is a true secondary sense in which the elect merit the salvation of the souls of others, and in which they expiate sin and avert its judgments. But it is by permission, by divine

> adoption, by participation, and in subordination to the one sole and complete redemption of Jesus Christ.[15]

The Pauline imperative of Colossians 1:24 calls all Christians to co-suffer with Jesus in the distribution of the graces of Redemption, or "*Redemption received.*" But Faber correctly points out the unique role of Mary Co-redemptrix with Jesus in "*Redemption accomplished*," or the historic obtaining of redemptive graces:

> She [Mary] co-operated with our Lord in the Redemption of the world in quite a different sense, a sense which can never be more than figuratively true of the saints. Her free consent was necessary to the Incarnation, as necessary as free will is to merit according to the counsels of God . . . . She consented to His Passion; and if she could not in reality have withheld her consent, because it was already involved in her original consent to the Incarnation, nevertheless, she did not in fact withhold it, and so He went to Calvary as her free-will offering to the Father . . . . Lastly, it was a co-operation of a totally different kind from that of the saints. Theirs was but the continuation and application of a sufficient redemption already accomplished, while

> hers was a condition requisite to the accomplishment of that redemption. One was a mere consequence of an event which the other actually secured, and which only became an event by means of it. Hence it was more real, more present, more intimate, more personal, and with somewhat of the nature of a cause in it, which cannot in any way be predicated of the co-operation of the saints.[16]

Faber goes on to enumerate three distinct rights of Mary to the title of Co-redemptrix:

> She has a right to it, first of all, because of her co-operation with our Lord in the same sense as the saints, but in a singular and superlative degree. She has a second right to it, which is peculiar to herself, because of the indispensable co-operation of her Maternity. She has a third right to it, because of her dolors . . . These last two rights are unshared by any other creature, or by all creatures collectively. They belong to the incomparable magnificence of the Mother of God.[17]

He concludes that "there is no other single word" which captures the full doctrine of Coredemption, in which the Mother of the Redeemer stands singularly above all the elect:

> In fact, there is no other single word in which the truth could be expressed; and, far off from His sole and sufficient redemption as Mary's co-operation lies, her co-operation stands alone and aloof from all the co-operation of the elect of God. This, like some other prerogatives of our Blessed Lady, cannot have justice done it by the mere mention of it. We must make it our own by meditation before we can understand all that it involves.[18]

Perhaps it is Faber's desire to translate the glory and sublimity of the truth of Co-redemptrix to the heart of the "common man," the "ordinary" London Catholic, that aids him in simplifying its truth in such palatable expressions. His staunch defense of the title is exceptional[19] as was his devotion to the Woman it represents.

For, in fact, "no other single word" captures the mystery of a creature playing such an unfathomable role in the buying back of all her fellow creatures, through a life of immaculate suffering with such infinite effects beyond the finiteness of the creature herself, all upon the condition that she gives back to the Divine the only part of her creaturehood that she truly possesses — her free will.

There is no other single word than Co-redemptrix

(try as we may through other Latinized neologisms or through longer theological phrases lacking the impact of that single word) to convey the co-operation of Mary "with Jesus" in the Redemption of the mankind.

During the first Vatican Council, the French Bishop, Jean Laurent, presents to the Council Fathers the following votum for the dogmatic definition of Mary Co-redemptrix. Although not accepted as mature for a dogmatic definition at the time, the votum nonetheless manifests the orthodoxy and significant ecclesial acceptance of the doctrine:

> The most Blessed Virgin Mary co-suffered and afterwards co-died with Christ suffering and dying for the salvation of mankind, made to divine justice most acceptable satisfaction . . . and became our Co-redemptrix with Christ — not because it was necessary (for the infinite merit of Christ abundantly sufficed), but by spontaneous and truly meritorious association.[20]

In the perennial struggle between the head and heart, between the intellect and love, it is Christian love which must predominate. The power of the saints and of the *sensus fidelium* is the power of Christian love in weakness (cf. 2 Cor 12:10). The theological mind must always guard itself against its greatest threat, that of intellectual pride (cf. 1 Cor 8:1), with the humble governors of the testimonies of saints and the Holy Spirit speaking through the universal Catholic faithful.

In a forward to a French work defending the Co-redemptrix title and doctrine by Jesuit father, P. Jeanjacquot († 1891), the prominent English Churchman, Cardinal Manning († 1892) writes strong words of admonition to those in theological and intellectual circles who seek to cast aspersion on the voices of the saints and the universal Christian faithful who profess love for their Mother as Co-redemptrix:

> There is nothing easier than to have a profound and a superficial mind at one and the same time; to be saturated with an undigested erudition and incapable of understanding the first principles of faith. Such is, to a very large extent, the state of some individuals who, while professing belief in the Incarnation and the Divine Word, refuse to style Mary Mother of God, and who raise their voices against the titles of co-redemptrix, co-operatrix, reparatrix, and mediatrix, after having misconstrued their meaning. The presumptuous audacity with which the language and the devotions, not only of ordinary Catholics, but also of the saints, have been censured by such authors, may have caused momentary alarm in some humble and timid souls. It is,

therefore, very opportune to place in their hands this excellent translation of a work which proves in a truly solid, clear and irrefutable manner, that, owing to the Word's Incarnation, Our Blessed Mother has received from her Divine Son a true right to all these titles. Hence, these titles which we give her are not metaphors but truths; they are not the expression of purely oratorical or poetical ideas, but the expression of true and living relations existing between her and her Divine Son, between her and us.[21]

Notes

[1] According to Laurentin's numbers (within the reasonable limitations of his study), the Co-redemptrix title is used twenty-four times to sixteen times for Redemptrix during the eighteenth century. In the nineteenth century, the Redemptrix title in used only by a few authors, while the usages of Co-redemptrix between 1850 and 1900 are "countless," certainly in the hundreds; cf. Laurentin, *Le Titre de Corédemptrice*, pp. 19-22 and footnote 76.

[2] De Montfort, *True Devotion to Mary*, n. 18.

[3] Categorized as merits *ex mera condignitate*; C. del Moral, *Fons Illimis theologiae scoticae marianae e paradiso lattices suos ubertim effundens*, Matriti, 1730, vol. 2, p. 420, n. 43.

[4] *Ibid.*, p. 385, n. 20.

[5] St. Alphonsus de Liguori, *Glorie di Maria,* ed. Rome, Poliglotta, 1878, P. 2, disc. 6, p. 395.

[6] Cf. Laurentin, *Le Titre de Corédemptrice*, p. 59, n. 126.

[7] St. Alphonsus de Liguori, *La Glorie di Marie, discorso sulla Salve Regina*, ch. 1, *Opera Ascetiche*, Rome, 1937.

[8] *Ibid.*

[9] *Ibid.*, pp. 138-139.

[10] Ven. John Cardinal Newman, *Certain Difficulties Felt by Anglicans . . .*, vol. 2, p. 78.

[11] Cf. F. W. Faber, *The Foot of the Cross or the Sorrows of Mary*, Peter Reilly, 1956 (originally published in 1858); cf. also Calkins, "Mary the Coredemptrix in the Writings of Frederick William Faber (1814-1863)," *Mary at the Foot of the Cross: Acts of the International Symposium on Marian Coredemption*, Franciscan Friars of the Immaculate, 2001, pp. 317-344.

[12] Faber, *The Foot of the Cross*, p. 370.

[13] *Ibid.*, pp. 370-371.

[14] John Paul II has used the term several times, for example in addressing the sick at the Hospital of the Brothers of St. John of God (Fatebenefratelli) on Rome's Tiber Island on April 5, 1981,

L'Osservatore Romano, English edition, April 13, 1981, p. 6; while addressing the sick after a general audience given January 13, 1982, *Inseg.*, V/1, 1982, 91 and during an address to the Bishops of Uruguay gathered in Montevideo concerning candidates for the priesthood, May 8, 1988, *L'Osservatore Romano*, English edition, May 30, 1988, p. 4. See also Chapter XIII, footnote 22.

[15] Faber, *The Foot of the Cross*, p. 372.

[16] *Ibid.*, pp. 372-374.

[17] *Ibid.*, p. 375.

[18] *Ibid.*, p. 377. Note: A little later in the nineteenth century, the prominent German theologian, Matthias Scheeben, will both defend and challenge the legitimacy of the title of Co-redemptrix in the same work. In a manner similar to Faber, Scheeben will distinguish the unique role of the Virgin in Redemption beyond all other human collaboration, and then substantiate the use of the Co-redemptrix title when it is specified "in Christ and by Christ": "The collaboration of Mary with the Redeemer in the redemptive sacrifice of Christ . . . is manifestly different from all other human collaboration both by its intimacy and by its efficacy. And that is why it is necessary to look on the effects of the sacrifice of Christ as co-acquired by Mary in this sacrifice and by this sacrifice. It can be said that Mary, in union with Christ (that is to say, by her collaboration with Him), made satisfaction to God for the sins of the world, merited grace, and consequently redeemed the world, in that she offered with Him the price of our Redemption. But it is permitted to say that, only by specifying expressly that it is in Christ and by Christ — that is to say, in the sacrifice of Christ and by the sacrifice of Christ, in so far as she co-offered this sacrifice. It is in this sense and in this way that correctly and without danger the Mother of the Redeemer can be called Co-redemptrix" (M. Scheeben, *Dogmatik*, Freiburg, 1882, vol. 3, p. 608).

Later in the same work, Scheeben will object to the title on the basis that the term, Redemption speaks of something that is specific only to the divine Redeemer, in the same way as the concept of the High Priesthood of Christ, a formally ordained priesthood in which Mary cannot share (cf. Scheeben, *Dogmatik*, English trans. by Geukers, B. Herder Book, 1947, pp. 217-227). But Scheeben himself points out that the Fathers did in fact predicate redemption and ransom to Mary: "It is a very ancient idea in the Church, expressed by numerous witnesses, rather, it is a definite dogma, proven by the Church's mode of reading the protogospel in the Vulgate, 'She shall crush thy head,' (Gen. 3:15) that the effects of Christ's redeeming death can and must be ascribed, in a very real sense, to His Mother as to their principle. Indeed, in the writings of the Fathers and the saints, almost all titles indicating Christ in His activity as Redeemer are ascribed, in a proportional and fitting sense, to the Mother of the Redeemer also. She is thus called salvatrix, reparatrix, restauratrix, liberatrix, reconciliatrix of the world, in fact also redemptrix, as well as salvation, liberation, reconciliation, propitiation, and redemption" (Scheeben, *Dogmatik*, p. 193).

The term, Redemption, to buy back, is more general in nature and meaning to the specific concept of formally ordained priesthood in Christ, which cannot include Mary as a formal sacrificial priest. The "back and forth" discussion of Co-redemptrix by Scheeben here, so uncharacteristic for this typically clear and certain theologian, perhaps indicates the possible influence of the Linz bishop who had condemned use of the title in that diocese. This condemnation was later reversed with the ecclesiastical use of the title sanctioned by the Holy Office under the pontificate of Pius X (cf. Hauke, "Mary, 'Helpmate of the Redeemer': Mary's Cooperation in Salvation as a Research Theme," *International Symposium on Marian Coredemption*, note 34; Scheeben, *Dogmatik*, p. 197, note 8).

[19] In light of so clear and generous a defense of the Co-redemptrix title by Faber, it is difficult to understand the comments of Fr. Laurentin that the "best of authors [during this period] use it [the Co-redemptrix title] with much hesitation and embarrassment. For example, Father Faber," cf. Laurentin, *Le Titre de Corédemptrice*,

p. 22; It is on occasions like this that the unquestionable historical and scholarly contribution contained in *Le Titre* is unfortunately compromised by a negative commentary on the doctrinal development that, once again, cannot be substantiated in the sources.

[20] J. Laurent, *Vota Dogmatica Concilio Vaticano proponenda*; cf. K. Moeller, *Leben und Briefe von Johannes Theodor Laurent*, Trier, 1889, vol. 3, p. 29: ex *Collectanea Francescana*, vol. 14, 1944, p. 280.

[21] Cf. Carol, "The Problem of Our Lady's Co-redemption," *The American Ecclesiastical Review*, vol. 123, 1950, p. 38.

Chapter XI

Popes of the Marian Age and Mary Co-redemptrix

Building upon the Scriptural and Traditional bedrock of over eighteen centuries of the story of the Co-redemptrix, the Vicars of Christ become the main impetuses for the complete development of this doctrine. The nineteenth and twentieth century papal pronouncements bring the doctrine, and eventually the title, to the ranks of the ordinary teaching of the Church's Magisterium — guided by the Holy Spirit and exercising the Petrine authority they alone possess.

So great is the Church's love of the Mother of God, so forthright is its articulation of the truth about her during this period, that it has been universally designated as the "Age of Mary." Generally dated from the 1830 "Miraculous Medal" apparitions of Our Lady of Grace to St. Catherine Labouré and extending to our own present day, this remarkable period of Church history has seen the declaration of two Marian dogmas, an explosion of Marian life, literature, art, and devotion, and has experienced exponentially more ecclesiastically approved Marian apparitions than at any other period in the Church's history.

It should not be surprising, therefore, to observe the remarkable Mariological development of doctrine and devotion to their Co-redemptive Mother taught by the Holy Fathers of the Marian Age.

This brings us to the question of what, precisely, constitutes the papal teaching of the ordinary Magisterium, the Church's authoritative teaching office?

The Second Vatican Council instructs us that a "loyal submission of will and intellect must be given, in a special way, to the authentic teaching authority of the Roman Pontiff, even when he does not speak *ex cathedra*."[1] This supreme teaching authority is "made known principally either by the character of the documents in question, or by the frequency with which a certain document is proposed, or by the manner in which a certain document is formulated" (*Lumen Gentium*, 25).

As we shall see, the "character" of the papal documents which articulate the doctrine of Mary Co-redemptrix include encyclical letters, the official channel of communication for the ordinary Magisterium, as well as other forms of papal teachings such as Apostolic letters, exhortations and general addresses (as well as the later ecumenical conciliar teachings of the Second Vatican Council). The truth of Mary Co-redemptrix has also been confirmed by the "frequency" of papal teaching of the Coredemption doctrine[2] and a repeated papal use of the Co-redemptrix title.[3] In fact, all the conciliar criteria for the ordinary teachings of the papal Magisterium are fulfilled by the nineteenth and twentieth century successors of Peter regarding Marian Coredemption and its title.[4]

It is of little wonder, therefore, that during this Marian Age, the Holy Fathers would bring greater precision and authoritative status to the story of Mary Co-redemptrix through their unprecedented papal testimony.[5] Building upon the scriptural, apostolic, patristic, and medieval theological foundations, they have validated its most prominent elements with a pneumatological guidance and protection possessed by no other teaching office on earth.

Remembering the principle that before the title, there must first be the role, we see this rule of priority pedagogically respected by the pontiffs, who begin by examining the role of Marian Coredemption, and then the role's expression in the actual Co-redemptrix title.

In his Apostolic Letter, *Ineffabilis Deus*, which defined the Immaculate Conception (1854), Blessed Pius IX makes reference to the Mother's Coredemption by recalling the early medieval declaration of her as the "Reparatrix of her first parents" and its scriptural origins in the Genesis 3:15 prophecy of her coredemptive battle with the Serpent: "Also did they declare that the most glorious Virgin was the Reparatrix of her first parents, the giver of life to posterity, that she was chosen before the ages, prepared for Himself by the Most High, foretold by God when he said to the Serpent, 'I will put enmities between you and the woman'— an unmistakable evidence that she has crushed the poisonous head of the Serpent"

(Bl. Pius IX, *Ineffabilis Deus*, Dec. 8, 1854).

In his encyclical, *Jucunda Semper*, Pope Leo XIII (1878-1903) teaches that Mary shared with Jesus the painful atonement on behalf of the human race in the depths of her soul: "When Mary offered herself completely to God together with her Son in the temple, she was already sharing with Him the painful atonement on behalf of the human race . . . [at the foot of the cross] she willingly offered Him up to divine justice, dying with Him in her heart, pierced by the sword of sorrow."[6]

The "Rosary Pope" of the nineteenth century also began a series of successive papal teachings which identify the Mother of the Lord as a "cooperatrix" (*co-operare*, "to work with") in the distribution of the graces of Redemption as a direct result of her cooperation in the obtaining of the graces of Redemption: "She who had been the cooperatrix in the sacrament of man's Redemption, would be likewise the cooperatrix in the dispensation of graces deriving from it."[7] Again, Our Lady is Mediatrix of all graces because she is first the Co-redemptrix; there is acquisition of grace before its distribution. The "Mother suffering" becomes the "Mother nourishing."

St. Pius X (1903-1914) carries on the papal tribute to Marian Coredemption in his first Marian encyclical, *Ad Diem Illum* (1904). In this famous text, the Pope of the Eucharist gives papal authority to the many previous theological testimonies to Mary's share in the merits of Redemption in light of her joint suffering with the Redeemer:

> Owing to the union of suffering and purpose existing between Christ and Mary, she merited to become most worthily the reparatrix of the lost world, and for this reason, the dispenser of all the favors which Jesus acquired for us by His death and His blood .... Nevertheless, because she surpasses all in holiness and in union with Christ, and because she was chosen by Christ to be His partner in the work of human salvation, she merits for us *de congruo*, as they say, that which Christ merited for us *de condigno*, and she is the principal dispenser of the graces to be distributed.[8]

In its traditional understanding, condign merit in its strict sense (*meritum de condigno ex toto rigore justitiae*) refers to a merit or "right to a reward" with an equality between the meritorious work and the reward, and also an equality between the person giving the reward and the person receiving the reward. Congruous merit (*meritum de congruo*) refers to a reward based both on the fittingness of a recompense for the act, and on the generosity of the one giving the reward.

The Catholic Catechism teaches that supernatural merit is both a gift of grace and a reward for man's co-working with God, which is founded upon God's free choice to associate man with his salvific work:

> With regard to God, there is no strict right to any merit on the part of man. Between God and us there is an immeasurable inequality, for we have received everything from him, our Creator.
>
> The merit of man before God in the Christian life arises from the fact that *God has freely chosen to associate man with the work of his grace.* The fatherly action of God is first on his own initiative, and then follows man's free acting through his collaboration, so that the merit of good works is to be attributed in the first place to the grace of God, then to the faithful. Man's merit, moreover, itself is due to God, for his good actions proceed in Christ, from the predispositions and assistance given by the Holy Spirit.[9]

Who, then, is more deserving of God's merit for collaborating in the work of salvation with Christ than the Mother Co-redemptrix? No other creature, human or angelic, chose to co-work with God in the redemptive plan more than the Immaculata, created full of grace and without sin by the Father of all mankind precisely for this very purpose.

St. Pius X validates on the authoritative level of the ordinary Magisterium that Mary merits for humanity in the order of "fittingness" or congruous merit, that which Jesus merits for us in the order of "justice" or strict condign merit. The Mother at Calvary obtains merit for humanity at least *de congruo*,[10] based on the appropriateness of recompense for her joint suffering with Jesus, coupled with the generosity of the Eternal Father for the Virgin Daughter's sacrifice of love and obedience offered to Him for the world's salvation.

The Magisterium's Use of the Co-redemptrix Title

The first usages of the Co-redemptrix title in the official pronouncements of the Roman Congregations also take place under the Magisterium of St. Pius X. Co-redemptrix is used three times by the Holy See in the initiatives of three Congregations of the Curia, and is thus contained in the publication of their official acts, *Acta Sanctae Sedis* (later to become *Acta Apostolicae Sedis*).

The first official use of Co-redemptrix comes on May 13, 1908, in a document by the Congregation of Rites. In positive response to a petition to raise the rank of the feast of the Seven Sorrows of Mary to a double rite of second class for the universal Church, the Congregation of Rites expresses its hope that "the devotion of the Sorrowful Mother may increase and the piety of the faithful and their gratitude toward the merciful Co-redemptrix of the human race may intensify."[11]

The Congregation of the Holy Office (currently, the Congregation for the Doctrine of the Faith) is the next congregation to use the term. On June 26, 1913, expressing the Congregation's satisfaction in adding the name of Mary to the name of Jesus in the indulgenced greeting, "Praised be Jesus and Mary" which is then responded to, "Now and forever," the official document signed by Cardinal Rampolla states: "There are those Christians whose devotion to the most favored among virgins is so tender as to be unable to recall the name of Jesus without the accompanying name of the Mother, our Co-redemptrix, the Blessed Virgin Mary."[12]

Six months later, the same Holy Office grants a partial indulgence for the recitation of a prayer of reparation to the Blessed Virgin (*Vergine benedetta*). The prayers ends with the words: "I bless thy holy Name, I praise thine exalted privilege of being truly Mother of God, ever Virgin, conceived without stain of sin, Co-redemptrix of the human race."[13]

In these instances, the Holy Office which is commissioned by the Church as the guardian of doctrinal orthodoxy, freely uses the Co-redemptrix term in a complementary reference to the Feast of Our Lady of Sorrows, which manifests its sense of familiarity with and confidence in the term itself. The same Dicastery then grants indulgenced graces to a prayer that identifies the role of Mary, Co-redemptrix of the human race, as a privilege worthy of blessing. The use of the title by the Congregation of Rites (currently the Congregation for

Divine Worship and the Discipline of the Sacraments) also speaks to the appropriateness of the title as part of authentic Catholic devotion.

It is, moreover, under the pontificate of St. Pius X that the First International Mariological Congress takes place in Rome in 1904 (in celebration of the fiftieth anniversary of the Dogma of the Immaculate Conception), where the theme of Mary Co-redemptrix dominates the Congress. The French theologian (later Cardinal) Alexis Lépicier († 1936) presents a paper which is soon published as a book entitled, *The Immaculate Mother of God, Co-redemptrix of the human race.*[14] In the text, Lépicier states that after the Mother of God, the title of Co-redemptrix is the most glorious that can be granted to the Virgin. Lépicier's contribution is favorably received by numerous theologians and Mariologists at the Rome congress.[15]

The following pontiff, Benedict XV (1914-1922) provides an invaluable contribution to the exactness of the doctrine of Coredemption as the unequivocal teaching of the papal Magisterium. In his classic text from the Apostolic Letter, *Inter Sodalicia* (1918) Pope Benedict articulates the Mother's co-suffering participation in the Passion, her immolation of her Son in appeasement of the Father's justice, and concludes with the explicit papal teaching that Mary "redeemed the human race together with Christ": "To such extent did [Mary] suffer and almost die with her suffering and dying Son; to such extent did she surrender her maternal rights over her Son for man's salvation, and immolated Him — insofar as she could —

in order to appease the justice of God, that we rightly say she redeemed the human race together with Christ."[16]

Upon the shoulders of these pontiffs and their official teachings on Coredemption, Pope Pius XI (1922-1939) becomes the *first pontiff to use the title of Co-redemptrix in papal addresses*.

The first occasion is on November 30, 1933, in a papal allocution to the pilgrims of Vicenza, Italy. Pastorally sensitive as well as doctrinally sound, Pius XI explains in this first papal usage of "Co-redemptrix" precisely why it is a legitimate term under which to invoke the Mother of the Redeemer: "By necessity, the Redeemer could not but associate [Italian, "*non poteva, per necessità di cose, non associare*"] his Mother in his work. For this reason we invoke her under the title of Coredemptrix. She gave us the Savior, she accompanied Him in the work of Redemption as far as the Cross itself, sharing with Him the sorrows of the agony and of the death in which Jesus consummated the Redemption of mankind."[17]

In this simple passage, Pope Pius XI gives the rationale for the Co-redemptrix title, in light of how the Redeemer could not "not" have associated his Mother within God's perfect providence in Redemption.[18]

During the 1934 Holy Year of Redemption, Pius XI repeats the Co-redemptrix title during the Lenten commemoration of Our Lady of Sorrows. *L'Osservatore Romano* reports the pontiff's remarks to Spanish pilgrims on that occasion: The Pope notes with joy that they have come to Rome to celebrate with him "not only the nineteenth centenary of the divine Redemption, but also the nineteenth centenary of Mary, the centenary of her Coredemption, of her universal maternity."[19] The Holy Father then exhorts the youth to: "follow the way of thinking and the desire of Mary most holy, who is our Mother and our Coredemptrix: they, too, must make a great effort to be coredeemers and apostles, according to the spirit of Catholic Action, which is precisely the cooperation of the laity in the hierarchical apostolate of the Church."[20]

In the following year, Pius XI for a third time invokes the Mother of Jesus as the Co-redemptrix in a radio broadcast, which the pontiff knew would reach far beyond the limits of a smaller papal audience in Rome, which would "carry weight and of universal outreach."[21] In his April 28, 1935 Radio Message for the closing of the Holy Year at Lourdes, Pius XI directly invokes the Mother as the "Co-redemptrix" who assisted the Lord in the offering of the "sacrifice of our Redemption": "O Mother of love and mercy who, when thy sweetest Son was consummating the Redemption of the human race on the altar of the cross, didst stand next to Him, suffering with Him as Coredemptrix . . . preserve in us, we beseech thee, and increase day by day the precious fruit of His redemption and thy compassion."[22]

Pope Pius XII (1939-1958) does not explicitly use the title, but repeatedly elucidates Coredemption's doctrinal teaching on the level of the ordinary Magisterium. In his encyclical, *Mystici Corporis* (1943), he states that the ancient

New Eve doctrine is properly fulfilled by Mary's Coredemption at Calvary, and that Mary as the "New Eve" offers Jesus to the Eternal Father, sacrificing with him on behalf of "all the children of Adam": "It was she who, always most intimately united with her Son, like a New Eve, offered Him up on Golgotha to the Eternal Father, together with the sacrifice of her maternal rights and love, on behalf of all the children of Adam, stained by the latter's shameful fall."[23]

During a May 13, 1946, radio message for pilgrims on the anniversary of the Fatima apparitions, Pius XII speaks of the Immaculate Virgin as the "co-operatrix" in association with the "King of Martyrs" in the "ineffable work of human Redemption":

> He, the Son of God, reflects on His heavenly Mother the glory, the majesty and the dominion of His kingship; for, having been associated with the King of Martyrs in the ineffable work of human Redemption as Mother and cooperatrix, she remains forever associated with Him, with an almost unlimited power, in the distribution of graces which flow from the Redemption. Jesus is King throughout all eternity by nature and by right of conquest; through Him, with Him and subordinate to Him, Mary is Queen by grace, by divine relationship, by right of conquest and by singular election.[24]

Note how eloquently this pontiff relates Mary's Coredemption with her Queenship, obtained by right of her victorious conquest with Christ the King in the restoration of grace. Pius XII is also reiterating the successive papal teaching that the Mother distributes the graces of Redemption as a direct result of her association with Christ in the work of Redemption through which the graces were acquired.

In his 1954 encyclical on Our Lady's Queenship (*Ad Caeli Reginam*), Pius XII uses his favored expression of "Associate" of the Redeemer[25] in referring to the Mother's share in Redemption. He cites the seventeenth century Jesuit mariologist, Suarez in attesting to her unique cooperation in Redemption: "Just as Christ, because He redeemed us, is by a special title our King and our Lord, so too is Blessed Mary [our Queen and our Mistress] because of the unique way in which she cooperated in our redemption."[26] In another allocution, the pontiff (now Venerable Pius XII) affirms the unity of the New Adam and the New Eve in making "satisfaction" for the guilt of the first Adam and Eve: "Are not Jesus and Mary the two sublime loves of the Christian people? Are they not the new Adam and the new Eve, whom the tree of the cross unites in sorrow and in love in order to make satisfaction for the guilt of our first parents in Eden?"[27]

What, then, can we conclude from the authoritative witness of the pontiffs of the Marian Age leading up to the Second Vatican Council? This brotherhood of remarkable Holy Fathers grants official papal approval to the doctrine of Mary Co-redemptrix and, by example and explanation, to the title of Mary Co-redemptrix. They confirm the Mother's merit[28] and satisfaction[29] at Calvary, her participation in the sacrifice,[30] and her sharing in the payment of the price for humanity's debt.[31] The popes of the Marian Age repeatedly use the new terminology applied to Mary, such as "co-operatrix"[32] and "co-redemptrix,"[33] and confirm her co-suffering and co-dying with Jesus at Calvary.[34]

In short, these Marian Age pontiffs bring to the official teachings of the papal Magisterium the best ideas and formulations on Coredemption, drawing from the deep reservoir of insights of the Church Fathers and Doctors, of John the Geometer, St. Bernard and Arnold, St. Albert and Tauler, the best of the seventeenth century Golden Age, and the mysticism of St. Catherine and St. Bridget of Sweden. Indeed, the mystical revelation from the lips of Our Lady herself through St. Bridget, which testifies that, "My son and I redeemed the world as with one heart,"[35] is affirmed with papal authority from the lips of Benedict XV, who testifies that Our Lady "redeemed the human race together with Christ."

Notes

[1] *Lumen Gentium*, 25.

[2] A number of citations have been found in the more extensive work by Msgr. Arthur B. Calkins, "The Mystery of Mary Coredemptrix in the Papal Magisterium," *Mary Co-redemptrix: Doctrinal Issue Today*, Queenship, 2002, pp. 25-92

[3] The criterion of repetition in regards to the papal use of the title of Co-redemptrix includes the six usages by John Paul II which will be examined in the next chapter.

[4] For the same application of conciliar criterion to Marian Coredemption specific to the Magisterium of John Paul II, cf. Calkins, "Pope John Paul II's Teaching on Marian Coredemption," *Mary Coredemptrix Mediatrix Advocate: Theological Foundations II*, Queenship, 1996, p. 145. Note: While the Co-redemptrix title has not been used in papal documents of a conciliar or encyclical character, its repetition (at least on nine occasions by Pius XI and John Paul II collectively) fulfills the conciliar criteria of "frequency" of papal teaching.

[5] For an extended treatment, cf. Calkins, "The Mystery of Mary Coredemptrix in the Papal Magisterium," pp. 25-92; Carol, "Our Lady's Coredemption," pp. 382-386; J. Schug, CAP., "Mary Coredemptrix: Her Title and Its Significance in the Magisterium of the Church," *Mary Coredemptrix Mediatrix Advocate: Theological Foundations*, Queenship, 1995, pp. 215-246.

[6] Leo XIII, Encyclical *Jucunda Semper.*

[7] Leo XIII, *ASS* 28, 1895-1896, pp. 130-131.

[8] St. Pius X, Encyclical *Ad Diem Illum*; *ASS* 36, p. 453.

[9] *Catechism of the Catholic Church*, nn. 2007-2008.

[10] Mary cannot merit condign merit in the strict sense, since there is obviously not an equality between the person of God and the created person of Mary, which is necessary to satisfy the second condition for strict condign merit. Only the God-man can receive merit in a relationship of strict justice for the redemptive act

performed at Golgotha, and within a relationship of equality between himself and his Eternal Father.

If there is not an equality between the persons giving the reward and receiving the reward, but still equality between the meritorious act and the reward, then this type of merit can be referred to as "*condign merit ex mera condignitate*" (cf. Carol, "Our Lady's Coredemption," p. 410; cf. also M. Llamera, O.P., *Alma Socia Christi*, Rome, 1951, vol. 1, p. 245 and M. Cuervo, O.P., "La cooperación de María en el misterio salud . . . ," *Estudios Marianos*, 1943, vol. 2, pp. 137-139). Several authors, in continuation of the position perhaps started by del Moral († 1731), support the general thesis that Mary did merit in the order of a condign merit as there was an equity between her coredemptive work and its recompense by God for all humanity, but obviously not in a strict sense of equality between her and God (cf. J. Lebon, "Comment je conçois, j'établis et je defends la doctrine de la Médiation mariale," *Ephemerides Theoligicae Lovanienses*, 1939, vol. 16, pp. 674-678; A. Fernández, O.P., "De Mediatione B. Virginis secundum doctrinam D. Thomae," *La Ciencia Tomista*, 1938, vol. 38, pp. 145-170; C. Balić, "Die sekundäre Mittlerschaft der Gottesmutter (Hat Maria die Verdienste Christi de condigno für uns mitverdient?)," *Wissenschaft und Weisheit*, 1937, vol. 4, pp. 1-22; L. Colomer, O.F.M., "Cooperación meritoria de la Virgen a la Redención," *Estudios Marianos*, 1943, vol. 2, pp. 155-177; M. Cuervo, *Ibid.*; J. A. de Aldama, S.J., "Cooperación de María a la Redención . . . ," *Estudios Marianos*, 1943, vol. 2, pp. 179-193; E. Sauras, O.P., "Causalidad de la cooperación de María . . . ," *Estudios Marianos*, 1943, vol. 2, pp. 319-358; F. Vacas, O.P., "María Corredentora pudo merecer de condigno ex condignitate," *Boletín Eclesiástico de Filipinas*, 1940, vol. 18, pp. 719-729; M. Llamera, O.P., "El mérito maternal corredentivo de María," *Estudios Marianos*, 1951, vol. 11, pp. 83-140; cf. also Llamera, *Alma Socia Christi*, vol. 1, pp. 243-255).

[11] *AAS* 1, 1908, p. 409.

[12] *AAS* 5, 1913, p. 364.

[13] *AAS* 6, 1914, p. 108.

[14] A. Lépicier, *L'Immacolata Madre di Dio, Corredentrice del genere umano*, Roma, 1905.

[15] *Ibid.*

[16] Benedict XV, Apostolic Letter *Inter Sodalicia*; *AAS* 10, pp. 181-182.

[17] Pius XI, *L'Osservatore Romano*, December 1, 1933, p. 1.

[18] Laurentin's exegetical questioning of the accuracy of this text, as well as the March 23, 1934 text, appears somewhat overstated (cf. Laurentin, *Le Titre de Corédemptrice*, p. 26). It is a basic fact that Pius XI used the Co-redemptrix title accompanied by an explanatory rationale for the title, in the office of Roman pontiff, in a document which has the character of a public address. How much deliberation came before its usage, based on a prepared text or the lack thereof, becomes rather questionable speculation. It is recorded in *L'Osservatore Romano* as the words of Pius XI explaining the use of the title Co-redemptrix with an explanatory rationale for its use. The objection raised by Laurentin is not immediately concerning the legitimate question of examining upon what level of papal authority is being used here, but rather whether it is an authentic papal allocution or not. It would not be advisable to use similar speculation to judge the merits of other papal allocutions, or even to question, for example, the status of papal allocutions previously prepared by a theological writer and not by the hand of the pontiff himself. In some cases, the spontaneous words of a pope manifest the true convictions of his mind and heart with even greater authenticity in manifesting his confidence and familiarity with, for example, the Co-redemptrix title.

Laurentin does conclude in the same document that because the term was "used or protected" by the two popes, the Co-redemptrix term does merit our respect and its legitimacy should not be attacked: "Used or protected by two popes, even in the most humble exercise of their supreme magisterium, the term henceforth requires our respect. It would be gravely presumptuous, at the very least, to attack its legitimacy" (Laurentin, *Le Titre de Corédemptrice*, pp. 27-28). But then he follows with the conclusion that "it would be inexact to say Rome positively recommends or encourages its use." Is the pope's own example in using the Coredemptrix title not in itself a positive recommendation or encouragement of its use, particularly within a papal address "carrying weight and universal outreach" (to quote Laurentin's own words)?

[19] Pius XI, *L'Osservatore Romano*, March 25, 1934, p. 1.

[20] *Ibid.*

[21] Cf. Laurentin, *Le Titre de Corédemptrice*, p. 27.

[22] Pius XI, *L'Osservatore Romano*, April 29-30, 1935, p. 1.

[23] Ven. Pius XII, Encyclical *Mystici Corporis*, June 29, 1943; *AAS* 35, 1943, p. 247.

[24] Ven. Pius XII, *Radio Message to Fatima*, May 13, 1946; *AAS* 38, p. 266.

[25] Ven. Pius XII; Encyclical *Ad Caeli Reginam*; *AAS* 46, 1954, p. 635.

[26] *Ibid.*, p. 634.

[27] Ven. Pius XII, *L'Osservatore Romano*, April 22-23, 1940, p. 1.

[28] Cf. St. Pius X, *Ad Diem Illum*.

[29] Cf. Ven. Pius XII, *AAS* 46, 1954, p. 635; cf. Benedict XV, *Inter Sodalicia*.

[30] Cf. Ven. Pius XII, *Mystici Corporis*; *AAS* 35, p. 247.

[31] Cf. Leo XIII, *Jucunda Semper*; Benedict XV, *Inter Sodalicia*; Ven. Pius XII, *L'Osservatore Romano*, April 22-23, 1940.

[32] Cf. Leo XIII, *ASS* 28, 1895-1896, pp. 130-131; Ven. Pius XII, *Radio Message to Fatima*.

[33] Cf. Magisteriums of Pius X and Pius XI.

[34] Cf. Leo XIII, *Jucunda Semper*; Benedict XV, *Inter Sodalicia*.

[35] St. Bridget, *Revelationes*, L. I, c. 35.

Chapter XII

The Council and Co-redemptrix

On January 25, 1959, "Good Pope" John XXIII, now Blessed, announces his desire to call an ecumenical council. The working preparations for the Second Vatican Council soon commence. On June 18 of that year, a circular letter is sent from Rome to all cardinals, archbishops, bishops, and general superiors of Religious families, followed on July 18 by a letter to Catholic universities and faculties of Theology. The purpose of the letters is to request from the future Council Fathers suggestions for the themes that should be eventually treated at the Council itself.[1]

These suggested topics are obtained during the antepreparatory period completed by spring of 1960.[2] The Secretary of the antepreparatory council then compiles a summary of the petitions and proposals from the bishops and prelates. Among these petitions, there are *approximately four hundred requests by bishops for a dogmatic definition of Our Lady's mediation, which included her cooperation in the Redemption, and particularly her role as Mediatrix of all graces.*[3] Approximately fifty bishops request a dogmatic definition of Mary specifically as the "Co-redemptrix."[4]

It is reported that the highest number of petitions

on any single issue that the future Council Fathers agree merit a conciliar statement is on Our Lady's mediation; the second largest number of petitions seeks a condemnation of communism; and the third issue of greatest agreement is the need for a solemn dogmatic definition on the Mother's role of universal mediation "with Jesus."[5]

The later direction for Vatican II, which is announced by Blessed John XXIII on the Council's opening day of October 11, 1962 (at that time, the feast of the Divine Maternity of Mary) will be "predominantly pastoral in character" and not dogmatic. Even so, the great quantity of "vota" or petitions for a dogmatic definition of the Mother's Coredemption and mediation is historically significant, for it is evidence of how greatly the Council Fathers love the universal Mother and seek to profess the whole truth about her role in salvation history.[6]

The first draft or "schema" on the Blessed Virgin Mary is presented to the Council Fathers on November 23, 1962. The schema is prepared by a subcommission of theologians and titled, "On the Blessed Virgin Mary, Mother of God and Mother of Men."[7] Little known is the fact *that the documentation contained in this first schema from the Second Vatican Council provides a beautiful synthesis of the history of the doctrine of Mary as "Co-redemptrix," from the New Eve doctrine of the Early Fathers to the rich teachings of the nineteenth and twentieth century papal Magisterium leading up to the Council.*

In the section which refers to the various titles in

which the cooperation of the Mother of God with Christ in the work of human Redemption is expressed,[8] the documentation offers the following substantiation of the legitimacy of the title of Co-redemptrix and its doctrine (which follows an extended notation in support of the New Eve tradition):

> All these things developed from the Pontiffs and the theologians, and a terminology was created in which Mary is soon called the "spiritual Mother of men, Queen of heaven and earth"; in other ways, "New Eve, Mediatrix, Dispensatrix of all graces," and indeed, "Co-redemptrix" . . . To that which pertains to the title, "Co-redemptrix," and "Associate of Christ the Redeemer," some things must be added.
>
> Already in the tenth century, the title of "Redemptrix" was used: "Holy Redemptrix of the world, pray for us." When in the fifteenth and sixteenth century, this familiar title was used, already an immediate cooperation of the Blessed Virgin in the work of our Redemption was recognized, and to the name, "Redemptrix" is added "co," and therefore the Mother of God was called, "Co-redemptrix," while Christ continued to be called, "Redeemer." From that time to the seventeenth century, the

> title Co-redemptrix was brought into use not only in devotional works of piety and holiness, but also in a great number of theological tracts.[9] This also pertains to the Roman pontiffs, as it has occurred in certain texts of St. Pius X and Pius XI . . . .[10]

The schema notation goes on to mention how Pope Pius XII used formulas such as "Associate of the Redeemer," "Noble Associate of the Redeemer," "Loving Associate of the Redeemer" and "Associate in the divine work of Redemption" without the specific term,[11] but also how the help of Mary "cum Iesu" in the economy of salvation is frequently praised by the supreme pontiffs. It subsequently quotes Pope Pius XI using the Co-redemptrix title on December 1, 1933, and proceeds to cite further references in support of the Co-redemptrix doctrine by Popes Leo XIII, Pius XI, and Pius XII. Its documentation even refers back to Pius VI in the eighteenth century, who condemns the thesis that unless a title of Mary is not explicitly contained in Scripture then it cannot be believed, even though approved by the Church and incorporated into its public prayer (*Auctorem fidei*, 1794).[12]

With such extensive documentation for Co-redemptrix and its doctrine in the Church history and papal teachings, why then was the title not used in the final version of the Marian schema which later appeared as Chapter Eight of *Lumen Gentium*?

One certain reason for the absence of the Co-redemptrix title in the final version of the conciliar treatment on the Blessed Virgin is the inclusion of a "prohibition" for the title written by a theological subcommittee in the form of an "Explanatory Note" (*Praenotanda*), which immediately follows the text of the original Marian schema as it was distributed to the Council Fathers. The subcommission's prohibition reads: "Certain expressions and words used by Supreme Pontiffs have been omitted, which, in themselves are absolutely true, but which may be understood with difficulty by separated brethren (in this case, Protestants). Among such words may be numbered the following: 'Co-redemptrix of the human race' [Pius X, Pius XI] . . . ."[13]

The theological commission's prohibition is not based in any way on concerns over the doctrinal legitimacy of Co-redemptrix, for the note unequivocally states that titles like "Co-redemptrix of the human race" which have been used by the popes are "in themselves absolutely true." But the term is prohibited, rather, due to the opinions of certain members of the subcommission that Co-redemptrix is a term that "may be understood" by Protestant Christians "with difficulty."

Is it not fair to examine the prohibition of the Co-redemptrix term in the light of the entire genus of Catholic terminology? One is compelled to consider what would happen to the entire Catholic theological tradition if all our theological titles of faith were to be measured by the same standard. Certainly, Catholic terms such as "transubstantiation," "papal infallibility" or even "Mother of God" would suffer, since these terms certainly run the danger of being "understood with difficulty" by our brother and sister Christians who are not in the full Catholic communion.

Nonetheless, the subcommission's prohibition is followed. Sadly, the issue of including the Co-redemptrix title in Vatican II's treatment on Mary, in spite of its documented Catholic Tradition and authority, and the numerous petitions for its inclusion during the antepreparatory phase, *is not permitted to reach the Council floor for discussion by the Council Fathers themselves*, among whom the wind of the Holy Spirit is blowing.

Even so, the Spirit does safeguard a true and bountiful testimony to his coredemptive Bride. The doctrine of Mary's suffering "with Jesus" receives its greatest and most explicit witness of authority by any ecumenical council in Church history.

Marian Coredemption in Lumen Gentium

Early in Chapter Eight of *Lumen Gentium*, the Fathers of Vatican II introduce the humble clarification and disclaimer that this chapter on the Blessed Virgin in no way constitutes a "complete doctrine on Mary." On the contrary, the Fathers encourage the "work of theologians" to further clarify those opinions which can be "lawfully retained" as propounded in Catholic schools regarding her:

> It [this sacred synod] does not, however,

> intend to give a complete doctrine on Mary, nor does it wish to decide those questions which the work of theologians has not yet fully clarified. Those opinions therefore may be lawfully retained which are propounded in Catholic schools concerning her who occupies a place in the Church which is highest after Christ and also closest to us (*Lumen Gentium*, 54).

It is evident to anyone willing to examine most any international mariological journal of the nineteen forties, fifties, and early sixties[14] that a dominant, probably the most dominant, Mariological topic being studied by theologians and being "propounded in Catholic schools" at the time is the doctrine of the Mother's Coredemption and mediation. This is why *any idea that the Second Vatican Council sought to put an end to the doctrinal development of Mary Co-redemptrix is simply an erroneous contradiction of the Council's own words and teachings.*

Four years prior to the commencement of the Council, the 1958 International Mariological-Marian Congress held at Lourdes is dedicated to the subject of the "Cooperation of the Blessed Virgin Mary and Church in the Redemption of Christ."[15] At this congress, a moral unanimity is reached by the theologians present in support of the doctrine of the Mother's unique cooperation in Christ's Redemption.[16] Mary Co-redemptrix is indeed being propounded in Catholic schools, mariological congresses, and seminaries, and with a vivacious appreciation of its doctrinal integrity.

The Council begins its theological treatment of Mary's Coredemption in section II of *Lumen Gentium*, titled "The Function of the Blessed Virgin in the Plan of Salvation" (LG, 55-59). Here they refer to the Old Testament prophecies of the Mother of the Redeemer, which is fulfilled in the new plan of salvation, when the Daughter Zion gives flesh to the Son of God to free man from sin:

> ...The earliest documents, as they are read in the Church and are understood in the light of a further and full revelation, bring the figure of a woman, Mother of the Redeemer, into a gradually clearer light. Considered in this light, she is already prophetically foreshadowed in the promise of victory over the serpent which was given to our first parents after their fall into sin (cf. Gen. 3:15). Likewise she is the virgin who shall conceive and bear a son, whose name shall be called Emmanuel (cf. Is. 7:14; Mic. 5:2-3; Mt. 1:22-23). She stands out among the poor and humble of the Lord, who confidently hope for and receive salvation from him. After a long period of waiting the times are fulfilled in her, the exalted Daughter of Sion and the new plan

> of salvation is established, when the Son of God has taken human nature from her, that he might in the mysteries of his flesh free man from sin.[17]

The document then quotes the ancient Fathers in articulating the Mother's active cooperation in the plan of salvation by citing the New Eve model and the principle of Recapitulation:

> The Father of mercies willed that the Incarnation should be preceded by assent on the part of the predestined mother, so that just as a woman had a share in bringing about death, so also a woman should contribute to life . . . Thus the daughter of Adam, Mary, consenting to the word of God, became the Mother of Jesus. Committing herself whole-heartedly and impeded by no sin to God's saving will, she devoted herself totally, as a handmaid of the Lord, to the person and work of her Son, under and with him, serving the mystery of redemption, by the grace of Almighty God. Rightly, therefore, the Fathers see Mary not merely as passively engaged by God, but as freely cooperating in the work of man's salvation through faith and obedience. For, as St Irenaeus says, she

> "being obedient, became the cause of salvation for herself and for the whole human race." Hence not a few of the early Fathers gladly assert with him in their preaching: "the knot of Eve's disobedience was untied by Mary's obedience: what the virgin Eve bound through her disbelief, Mary loosened by her faith." Comparing Mary with Eve, they call her "Mother of the living," and frequently claim: "death through Eve, life through Mary."[18]

We see here how the Council teaches that the Mother "devoted herself totally, as a handmaid of the Lord, to the person and the work of her Son, under him and with him, serving the mystery of Redemption." This is the Mother "with Jesus" in the work of Redemption — unequivocal and straightforward. We have here Vatican II's certain teaching of the legitimacy of Marian Coredemption. But this is only the beginning.

The Council Fathers refer to the Mother's singular co-operation which lasts throughout her earthly life: "The work of the Mother with the Son in the work of salvation is made manifest from the time of Christ's virginal conception up to his death" (LG, 57). They then summarize the first years of this cooperation, from the Visitation, to the miraculous birth, to the coredemptive prophecy at the Presentation, to the Virgin's sorrow at being separated from her son at the Temple (cf. LG, 57).

The Council's most profound testimony to Coredemption comes in number 58 of *Lumen Gentium*. Substantiated by the papal teaching which led up to the Council, the Fathers synthesize the previous ordinary teachings of the Magisterium regarding Mary's co-suffering with Jesus at Calvary:

> In the public life of Jesus Mary appears prominently; at the very beginning when at the marriage feast of Cana, moved with pity, she brought about by her intercession the beginning of miracles of Jesus the Messiah (cf. Jn. 2:1-11). In the course of her Son's preaching she received the words whereby, in extolling a kingdom beyond the concerns and ties of flesh and blood, he declared blessed those who heard and kept the word of God (cf. Mk. 3:35; par. Lk. 11:27-28) as she was faithfully doing (cf. Lk. 2:19; 51). Thus the Blessed Virgin advanced in her pilgrimage of faith, and faithfully persevered in her union with her Son unto the cross, where she stood, in keeping with the divine plan, enduring with her only begotten Son the intensity of his suffering, associated herself with his sacrifice in her mother's heart, and lovingly consenting to the immolation of this victim which was born of her. Finally, she was

> given by the same Christ Jesus dying on the cross as a mother to his disciple, with these words: "Woman, behold thy son" (Jn. 19:26-27).

Enduring with Jesus his suffering; associating herself with his sacrifice; consenting to his immolation as Victim. Co-suffering; co-sacrificing; co-satisfying; co-redeeming. Does the Council not rally behind the best of the Tradition of Coredemption?

To further elaborate their teaching on Marian Coredemption, the Council summarizes again Mary's lifelong work of sharing the sufferings of the Redeemer and teaches that her sharing in the restoration of the supernatural life with Christ is the foundation for her role as the spiritual mother of all peoples. Taken up to heaven, Mary becomes the maternal Mediatrix of the "gifts of eternal salvation," but without any loss to the dignity of efficacy of Jesus, the one Mediator:

> The predestination of the Blessed Virgin as Mother of God was associated with the incarnation of the divine word: in the designs of divine Providence she was the gracious mother of the divine Redeemer here on earth, and above all others and in a singular way the generous associate and humble handmaid of the Lord. She conceived, brought forth, and nourished

Christ, she presented him to the Father in the temple, shared her Son's sufferings as he died on the cross. Thus, in a wholly singular way she cooperated by her obedience, faith, hope and burning charity in the work of the Savior in restoring supernatural life to souls. For this reason she is a mother to us in the order of grace.

This motherhood of Mary in the order of grace continues uninterruptedly from the consent which she loyally gave at the Annunciation and which she sustained without wavering beneath the cross, until the eternal fulfilment of all the elect. Taken up to heaven she did not lay aside this saving office but by her manifold intercession continues to bring us the gifts of eternal salvation. By her maternal charity, she cares for the brethren of her Son, who still journey on earth surrounded by dangers and difficulties, until they are led into their blessed home. Therefore the Blessed Virgin is invoked in the Church under the titles of Advocate, Helper, Benefactress, and Mediatrix. This, however, is so understood that it neither takes away anything from nor adds anything to the dignity and efficacy of Christ the one Mediator.[19]

Without question, the Second Vatican Council's testimony to the story of the Co-redemptrix is both doctrinally generous and theologically profound. Without using the title, it extensively teaches the doctrine — the truth without the name.

And yet the doctrine of Marian Coredemption and the title of Mary Co-redemptrix have an essential, ontological, revelational connection. They cannot be artificially separated. If one accepts the doctrine, as does the Second Vatican Council, then one must accept the truth of the title, which finds its source, its being, its history in the doctrine. *To state, therefore, that Vatican II did not teach the doctrine of Mary Co-redemptrix is an error of history and a violation of truth.*

The Second Vatican Council does not use the Co-redemptrix title "absolutely true in itself,"[20] but nevertheless professes the doctrine, which is the true mother of the title. The Catholic doctrine of Mary "with Jesus, from the Annunciation to Calvary" is the authoritative teaching of the Second Vatican Ecumenical Council. Its title, for the historical moment, is left out. But this moment of silence will soon pass with the Marian pontificate of John Paul II.

On June 4, 2002, Theologian of the Papal Household, Fr. Georges Cottier, O.P., publishes an article in the Vatican paper, *L'Osservatore Romano*, titled, "The Coredemption."[21] In this article, the papal theologian defends the legitimate use of the title of Co-redemptrix in light of the teachings of the Second Vatican Council. He also voices an authentic interpretation of the Council's doctrinal teachings on Mary's Coredemption:

> The Council's text, which we have quoted, strongly emphasizes this: Beneath the cross, Mary suffers deeply with her only born Son, she joins in his sacrifice with maternal love; lovingly consenting to the immolation of the victim generated by her: what could these words mean if not that Mary plays an active role in the mystery of the Passion and the work of redemption? The Council itself clarifies this . . . .
>
> Can we add to the title Mediatrix that of co-redemptrix? In the light of the above, the answer is affirmative.[22]

Notes

[1] Cf. G. M. Besutti, O.S.M., *Lo Schema Mariano al Concilio Vaticano II*, Edizioni Marianum, 1966, p. 17.

[2] 1998 responses were received which represented seventy-seven percent of those asked for suggestions, cf. Besutti, *Ibid*.

[3] Besutti states the number of bishops for the definition of Mary's Mediation was over 500, cf. Besutti, *Ibid*.; Cf. also A. Escudero Cabello, *La cuestión de la mediación mariana en la preparation del Vaticano II*, Rome, 1997, pp. 86-92 ; O'Carroll, *Theotokos*, p. 352.

[4] *Relationes*, Vatican Press, 1963, as quoted by O'Carroll, *Theotokos*, p. 308; cf. also Calkins, "The Mystery of Mary Coredemptrix in the Papal Magisterium," p. 36.

[5] Cf. O'Carroll, "Vatican II," *Theotokos*, p. 352.

[6] Cf. Chapter IV, note 11.

[7] Besutti, *Lo Schema Mariano*, p. 22; cf. also C. Balić, O.F.M., "La Doctrine sur la Bienheureuse Vierge Marie Mère de l'Eglise, et la Constitution "Lumen Gentium" du Concile Vatican II," *Divinitas*, vol. 9, 1965, p. 464.

[8] "De Beata Maria Vergine Matre Dei et Matre Hominum," Section 3, note 16, *Acta Synodalia Concilii Oecumenici Vaticani Secundi*, Typis Polyglottis Vaticanis, 1971, vol. 1. pt. 4. The relevant section of note 16, due to its importance in understanding how secure was the Co-redemptrix title and teaching at the time when the first schema was written, is here given in its Latin original:

> Quae omnia evoluta sunt a Theologis et a Summis Pontificibus, et creata est nomenclatura, ubi Maria vocatur mox *Mater spiritualis hominum*, mox *Regina caeli et terrae*, alia vice *Nova Heva, Mediatrix, Dispensatrix omnium gratiarum*, immo et *Corredemptrix*. Quod attinet ad titulum "Regina" cf. notam (14); quoad titulum "Mater spiritualis," "Mater hominum" cf. notam (12); quoad titulum

"Corredemptrix," Socia Christi Redemptoris" hic quaedam adiungenda sunt:

Iam saeculo x occurrit titulis *Redemptrix*: "Sancta redemptrix mundi, ora pro nobis." Quando saeculo xv et xvi hic titulus usitatus evadit, et iam percipitur immediata cooperatio B. Virginis in opere nostrae redemptionis, vocabolo "Redemptrix" additur "con," et ita Mater Dei nuncupatur "corredemptrix," dum Christus "Redemptor" appellari pergit. Inde a saeculo xvii, titulus "Corredemptrix" communissime usurpatur non solum in operibus pietati ac devotioni inservientibus, verum etiam in quamplurimis tractatibus theologicis [cf. Carol, J., *De corredemptione Beatae Virginis Mariae*, Romae, 1950, p. 482].

Quod vero attinet ad Romanos Pontifices, occurrit in quibusdam textibus S. Pii X et Pii XI, in contextibus minoris ponderis: cf. ASS 41(1908) p. 409; AAS 6 (1914) pp. 108 s.; *L'Osserv. Rom.*, 29-30 apr. 1935.

Pius XII consulto vitare voluit hanc expressionem adhibendo frequenter formulas "Socia Redemptoris," "Generosa Redemptoris Socia," "Alma Redemptoris Socia," "Socia in Divini Redemptoris opere."

Consortium Mariae cum Iesu in oeconomia nostrae salutis saepe saepius a Summis Pontificibus extollitur: "ad magnam Dei Matrem eamdemque reparandi humani generis consortem" [Leo XIII, Const. Apost. *Ubi primum*, 2 febr. 1898: Acta Leonis XIII, XVIII, p. 161];

Pius XI, Alloc. *peregrinantibus e diocesi Vicent.*: *L'Osser. Rom.* 1 dec. 1933: "Il Redentore non poteva, per necessità di cose, non associare la Madre Sua alla Sua opera, e per questo noi la invochiamo col titolo *Corredentrice* . . . ";

Pius XII, Litt. Encycl. *Ad caeli Reginam*, 11 oct. 1954: AAS 46 (1954) p. 634: "Si Maria, in spirituali procuranda salute cum Iesu Christo, ipsius salutis principio, ex Dei placito *sociata* fuit . . . . " Praeter titulos allatos adsunt quamplurimi alii, quibus a christifidelibus Maria salutatur.

Leo XIII, Litt. Encycl. *Supremi Apostolatus*, 1 sept. 1883: Acta Leonis XIII, III, p. 282: "Veteris et recentioris aevi historiae, ac sanctiores Ecclesiae fasti publicas privatasque ad Deiparam obsecrationes vota commemorant, ac vicissum praebita per Ipsam auxilia partamque divinitus tranquillitatem et pacem. Hinc insignes illi tituli, quibus Eam catholicae gentes christianorum Auxiliatricem, Opiferam, Solatricem, bellorum potentem Victricem, Paciferam consalutarunt."

Cf. Pius VI, Const. *Auctorem fidei*, 28 aug. 1794 [*Documentos Marianos*, n. 230]: "Item [doctrina] quae vetat, ne imagines, praesertim beatae Virginis, ullis titulis distinguantor, praeter denominationibus, quae sint analogae mysteriis, *de quibus in sacra Scriptura expressa fit mentio*; quasi nec adscribi possent imaginibus piae aliae denominationes, quas vel in ipsismet publicis precibus Ecclesia probat et commendat: temeraria, piarum aurium offensiva, *venerationi beatae praesertim Virgini debitae iniuriosa*."

[9] Here the documentation refers to "J. B. Carol, *De corredemptione Beatae Virginis Mariae*, Romae, 1950, p. 482."

[10] The note then cites: "cf. St. Pius X and Pius XI, in contexts of minor importance, cf. ASS 41 (1908), p. 409; AAS 6 (1914) pp. 108 s.; *L'Osservatore Romano*, 29-30, April, 1935."

[11] "De Beata Maria Vergine Matre Dei et Matre Hominum," Section

3, note 16, *Acta Synodalia Concilii Oecumenici Vaticani Secundi*, Typis Polyglottis Vaticanis, 1971, vol. 1. pt. 4.

[12] Although this documentation is not included in the final version of *Lumen Gentium*, Chapter 8, its presence in the first Marian schema given to the Council Fathers testifies strongly to its unquestionable foundation in Catholic Tradition and the ordinary teachings of the papal Magisterium.

[13] *Acta Synodalia Concilii*, vol. 1. pt. 4; cf. Besutti, *Lo Schema Mariano*, p. 41. Original Latin from Praenotanda reads: "Omissae sunt expressions et vocabula quaedam a Summis Pontificibus adhibita, quae, licet in se verissima, possent difficilius intelligi a fratribus separatis (in casu protestantibus). Inter alia vocabula adnumerari queunt sequential: 'Corredemptrix humani generis' [S. Pius X, Pius XI] . . . ."

[14] For example, cf. the great quantities of books reviewed and articles published on Marian Coredemption and mediation during this time period as contained in *Editiones Academie Marianae Internationalis*; *Ephemerides Mariologicae*; *Études Mariales*; *Marian Studies*; *American Ecclesiastical Review*, etc..

[15] *Maria et Ecclesia, Acta Congressus Mariologici-Mariani in Civitate Lourdes Anno 1958 Celebrati*, Romae, Academia Mariana Internationalis, Via Merulana, 24.

[16] *Ibid.*

[17] *Lumen Gentium*, 55.

[18] *Ibid.*, 56.

[19] *Ibid.*, 61-62.

[20] Cf. Explanatory note of theological subcommission in Besutti, *Lo Schema Mariano*, p. 41.

[21] G. Cottier, O.P., *L'Osservatore Romano*, Italian edition, June 4, 2002.

[22] *Ibid.* Note: During the Congregation for the Clergy's International Teleconference of May 28, 2003, chaired by its Prefect Cardinal Castrillón Hoyos, theologian and *L'Osservatore Romano* contributor, Fr. Jean Galot, S.J. offered yet another defense of the title of Co-redemptrix and its basis in the teachings of the Second Vatican Council which was promulgated throughout the world by this

Vatican congregation:

"Mary's cooperation in the work of salvation was already apparent in her consent to the Incarnation, but would only achieve its fullness when the doctrine of the redeeming sacrifice was clarified. For a long time Mary's actual intervention in this sacrifice was not taken into consideration: Mary could be called Redeemer, in the sense that as the mother of the Redeemer she had given the world a Saviour.

During the Middle Ages a doctrinal meditation concerning the sacrifice and meaning of Mary's participation in the Calvary drama also developed. So as to explain this participation that emphasized the suffering experienced by a mother in unity with the Son, Mary was no longer described as a Redeemer, but as the Co-redemptrix [original Italian, *Corredentrice*], because in suffering with the Saviour she had become associated with His redeeming work. Co-redemption means cooperating in redemption. It does not represent a likeness between Mary and Christ, because Christ is not the co-Saviour but the one and only Saviour. Mary is not the Redeemer but a Co-redemptrix [*Corredentrice*] , because she joined Christ in the offering of His Passion. In this manner the principle of the uniqueness of the Mediator is safeguarded: 'There is only one mediator between God and men, Jesus Christ, who is a man like them, and gave Himself as a ransom for them all' (1 Tim 2,5).

The Council denies that this uniqueness is endangered by Mary's mediating presence. Attributing to the Blessed Virgin the titles of Protectress, Helper, Rescuer, Mediatress, affirms that 'the unique mediation of the Redeemer does not exclude but rather gives rise to a manifold cooperation which is but a sharing in this one source' (62). The title of Co-redemptrix [*Corredentrice*] cannot therefore appear as a threat to Christ's sovereign power, because it is from this power that it emanates and finds its energy. The Council's words are clear: 'The maternal duty of Mary toward men in no way obscures or diminishes this unique mediation of Christ, but rather shows His power. For all the salvific influence of the Blessed

Virgin on men originates, not from some inner necessity, but from the divine pleasure. It flows forth from the superabundance of the merits of Christ, rests on His mediation, depends entirely on it and draws all its power from it. In no way does it impede, but rather does it foster the immediate union of the faithful with Christ' (60) . . .

The Council especially emphasizes Mary's participation in the sacrifice of the crucifixion: 'After this manner the Blessed Virgin advanced in her pilgrimage of faith, and faithfully persevered in her union with her Son unto the cross, where she stood, in keeping with the divine plan (see Jn 19:25) grieving exceedingly with her only begotten Son, uniting herself with a maternal heart with His sacrifice, and lovingly consenting to the immolation of this Victim which she herself had brought forth . . . .' In this tragedy Mary recognized a divine plan: that of Redemption.

The Vatican Council observed that the origins of Mary's destiny as the mother of God were predestined ever since eternity and that as the alma mater of the divine Saviour she was 'a totally exceptional generous companion' and 'humble handmaid of the Lord.' Her entire life was 'Co-redemption': 'She conceived, brought forth and nourished Christ. She presented Him to the Father in the temple, and was united with Him by compassion as He died on the Cross. In this singular way she cooperated by her obedience, faith, hope and burning charity in the work of the Saviour in giving back supernatural life to souls' (61). It is to this cooperation that Mary's supernatural gifts were all committed, qualities that were to be communicated to mankind."

Chapter XIII

The Pope of Mary Co-redemptrix

In witnessing to most every aspect of the story of Mary Co-redemptrix, John Paul II, the "Totus Tuus" Pope, has exceeded all papal predecessors. The quantity of such testimonies is vast; their depth profound; their love inspired.

As if before a wine cellar full of extraordinary wines, we do not have the opportunity to taste and appreciate every teaching of Pope John Paul concerning his Mother Co-redemptrix.[1] Rather, let us offer some of his most exceptional.

John Paul II and Usages of Co-redemptrix

John Paul II's official and repeated use of the title, Co-redemptrix quickly remedies the silence at the Council. Within his first years as Christ's Vicar, the Pope invokes the Immaculate Mother as "Co-redemptrix" on repeated occasions and makes whole again the relationship between the doctrine and the title. The title is legitimate, and the Holy Father expresses his conviction about this.

On September 8, 1982, Feast of the Birth of Mary, within the context of a papal address to the sick (who so much need to know the power of co-redemptive suffering), John Paul calls Mary the "Co-redemptrix of humanity" for the first time: "Mary, though conceived and born without the taint of sin, participated in a marvelous way in the sufferings of her divine Son, in order to be Coredemptrix of humanity."[2]

As is well known, John Paul does not celebrate his own birthday of May 18, but rather his "name day" on November 4, the feast of St. Charles Borromeo, after whom he is named "Karol." On this day in 1984 the Pope once again calls his Mother the "Co-redemptrix" in a general audience:

> To Our Lady — the Coredemptrix — St. Charles turned with singularly revealing accents. Commenting on the loss of the twelve-year-old Jesus in the Temple, he reconstructed the interior dialogue that could have run between the Mother and the Son, and he added, "You will endure much greater sorrows, O blessed Mother, and you will continue to live; but life will be for you a thousand times more bitter than death. You will see your innocent Son handed over into the hands of sinners . . . You will see him brutally crucified between thieves; you will see his holy side pierced by the cruel thrust of a lance; finally, you will see the blood that you gave him spilling.

> And nevertheless you will not be able to die!" (From the homily delivered in the Cathedral of Milan the Sunday after the Epiphany, 1584).[3]

The next usage of the Co-redemptrix title by the Holy Father is his most important to date. At a Marian sanctuary in Guayaquil, Ecuador, on January 31, 1985, Pope John Paul II delivers a homily in which he professes the Co-redemptrix title within a penetrating theological commentary of scriptural and conciliar teaching on Coredemption:

> Mary goes before us and accompanies us. The silent journey that begins with her Immaculate Conception and passes through the "yes" of Nazareth, which makes her the Mother of God, finds on Calvary a particularly important moment. There also, accepting and assisting at the sacrifice of her son, Mary is the dawn of Redemption; ... Crucified spiritually with her crucified son (cf. Gal. 2:20), she contemplated with heroic love the death of her God, she "lovingly consented to the immolation of this Victim which she herself had brought forth" (*Lumen Gentium*, 58) ....
>
> In fact, at Calvary she united herself with the sacrifice of her Son that led to

> the foundation of the Church; her maternal heart shared to the very depths the will of Christ "to gather into one all the dispersed children of God" (Jn. 11:52). Having suffered for the Church, Mary deserved to become the Mother of all the disciples of her Son, the Mother of their unity . . . .
>
> The Gospels do not tell us of an appearance of the risen Christ to Mary. Nevertheless, as she was in a special way close to the Cross of her Son, she also had to have a privileged experience of his Resurrection. In fact, Mary's role as Coredemptrix did not cease with the glorification of her Son.[4]

The Guayaquil homily by the Vicar of Christ cannot be dismissed as either marginal or devoid of doctrinal weight.[5] "Spiritually crucified with her crucified son . . ."; "she united herself with the sacrifice of her Son that led to the foundation of the Church . . ."; "her role as Co-redemptrix did not cease with the glorification of her Son . . ." — all of these declarations constitute sublime confessions to the doctrine of Mary Co-redemptrix. They are packed with doctrinal depth and conviction by the Holy Father, to whom the believing Catholic heart should assent with obedience, thanksgiving, and awe.

Only a few months later, John Paul confirms once again the legitimacy of Co-redemptrix. On Palm Sunday, during World Youth Day, the Holy Father addresses his "favorites," his beloved youth, and invokes the aid of Mary under the title of "the Co-redemptrix":

> At the Angelus hour on this Palm Sunday, which the Liturgy calls also the Sunday of the Lord's Passion, our thoughts run to Mary, immersed in the mystery of an immeasurable sorrow.
>
> Mary accompanied her divine Son in the most discreet concealment, pondering everything in the depths of her heart. On Calvary, at the foot of the Cross, in the vastness and in the depth of her maternal sacrifice, she had John, the youngest Apostle, beside her . . . .
>
> May Mary our Protectress, the Co-redemptrix, to whom we offer our prayer with great outpouring, make our desire generously correspond to the desire of the Redeemer.[6]

Again in context of the sick, (this time to volunteers of Lourdes) on March 24, 1990, the Pope calls upon the aid of Mary under the title "Co-redemptrix": "May Mary most holy, Co-redemptrix of the human race beside her Son, always give you courage and confidence!"[7]

In commemorating the sixth centenary of the canonization of St. Bridget of Sweden (October 6, 1991), the Holy Father uses "Co-redemptrix" as a title and role understood by this fourteenth century mystic whose revelations did so much to stimulate the medieval development of the doctrine:

> Birgitta looked to Mary as her model and support in the various moments of her life. She spoke energetically about the divine privilege of Mary's Immaculate Conception. She contemplated her astonishing mission as Mother of the Saviour. She invoked her as the Immaculate Conception, Our Lady of Sorrows, and Coredemptrix, exalting Mary's singular role in the history of salvation and the life of the Christian people.[8]

Clearly, the *Totus Tuus Pope affirms the authenticity of the Co-redemptrix title within the Church, both in the context of doctrinal treatments and in the order of prayerful invocation by the Church.*

John Paul II's contribution to the doctrinal advancement of Marian Coredemption is no less stellar. During the Marian month of May in 1983, the Successor of Peter highlights the Immaculate Virgin's association with Christ as the "highest model of cooperation," which is begun with her "yes" to the work of Redemption at the Annunciation:

> Dearest brothers and sisters, in the month of May we raise our eyes to Mary, the woman who was associated in a unique way in the work of mankind's reconciliation with God. According to the Father's plan, Christ was to accomplish this work through his sacrifice. However, a woman would be associated with him, the Immaculate Virgin who is thus placed before our eyes as the highest model of cooperation in the work of salvation. . . .
>
> The "Yes" of the Annunciation constituted not only the acceptance of the offered motherhood, but signified above all Mary's commitment to service of the mystery of the Redemption. Redemption was the work of her Son; Mary was associated with it on a subordinate level. Nevertheless, her participation was real and demanding. Giving her consent to the angel's message, Mary agreed to collaborate in the whole work of mankind's reconciliation with God, just as her Son would accomplish it.[9]

On the Feast of Corpus Christi, June 5, 1983, the Holy Father again underlines Our Lady's active part in the one Redemptive Sacrifice, which is continued in every Mass. In this sacrifice, Mary "offered him and she offered herself to the Father," and as a result, every Mass puts us in intimate communion "with her, the Mother":

> Born of the Virgin to be a pure, holy and immaculate oblation, Christ offered on the Cross the one perfect Sacrifice which every Mass, in an unbloody manner, renews and makes present. In that one Sacrifice, Mary, the first redeemed, the Mother of the Church, had an active part. She stood near the Crucified, suffering deeply with her Firstborn; with a motherly heart she associated herself with his Sacrifice; with love she consented to his immolation (cf. *Lumen Gentium*, 58; *Marialis Cultus*, 20): she offered him and she offered herself to the Father. Every Eucharist is a memorial of that Sacrifice and that Passover that restored life to the world; every Mass puts us in intimate communion with her, the Mother, whose sacrifice "becomes present" just as the Sacrifice of her Son "becomes present" at the words of consecration of the bread and wine pronounced by the priest.[10]

In the same year (December 7, 1983), John Paul II elucidates the crucial pre-requisite for the Mother's coredemptive mission as her Immaculate Conception (a truth of doctrinal interconnectedness which merits greater contemporary appreciation): "We must above all note that Mary was created immaculate in order to be better able to act on our behalf. The fullness of grace allowed her to fulfill perfectly her mission of collaboration with the work of salvation; it gave the maximum value to her cooperation in the sacrifice. When Mary presented to the Father her Son nailed to the cross, her painful offering was entirely pure."[11]

In the 1984 Apostolic Letter, *Salvifici Doloris* ("On the Christian Meaning of Human Suffering"), the Holy Father delivers an extraordinary teaching on the sufferings of Mary at Calvary:

> It is especially consoling to note — and also accurate in accordance with the Gospel and history — that at the side of Christ, in the first and most exalted place, there is always His Mother through the exemplary testimony that she bears by her whole life to this particular Gospel of suffering. In her, the many and intense sufferings were amassed in such an interconnected way that they were not only a proof of her unshakable faith but also a contribution to the Redemption of all .... It was on Calvary that Mary's suffering, beside the suffering of Jesus, reached an intensity which can hardly be imagined from a human point of view but which was mysteriously and

> supernaturally fruitful for the Redemption of the world. Her ascent of Calvary and her standing at the foot of the cross together with the beloved disciple were a special sort of sharing in the redeeming death of her Son.[12]

The Pope confirms the participation of the Co-redemptrix not only in the distribution of the graces of Calvary, but also *in the obtaining of universal redemptive graces*, when he declares that the many and intense sufferings were amassed in such a way that they were a "contribution to the Redemption of all."[13] Moreover his description that the Mother's sufferings at Calvary "reached an intensity which can hardly be imagined from a human point of view," attests to the extreme human limits of suffering for the Immaculate Heart of Mary, who watches and consents to the violent immolation of her innocent son, who is also God, so that humanity may be bought back. Because this unique sharing in the redeeming death of Christ is "supernaturally fruitful for the Redemption of the world," the Immaculate One willingly suffers in love for all mankind.

To the young pilgrims from Vicenza (reminiscent of Pius XI's first use of Co-redemptrix to the Vicenza pilgrims in 1933[14]), John Paul elaborates extemporaneously that with the death of Jesus on the cross, Mary's "very self, her heart, her motherhood," were likewise "crucified" in the greatest "dark night" of human history: "... when Jesus died on the cross, her very self, her heart, her motherhood, all was crucified. When I wrote the Encyclical *Redemptoris Mater* I compared this moment in Mary's life to a dark night, darker than all the nights which the souls of mystics have experienced throughout the Church's history."[15]

The teaching of John Paul's ordinary Magisterium in the 1995 encyclical, *Evangelium Vitae*, acknowledges the lifelong "yes" of the Co-redemptrix given at the Annunciation which reaches its fulfillment at Calvary, where Mary "offers Jesus" so as to "receive and beget" his disciples as her spiritual children:

> "Standing by the cross of Jesus" (Jn. 19:25), Mary shares in the gift which the Son makes of himself: she offers Jesus, gives him over, and begets him to the end for our sake. The "yes" spoken on the day of the Annunciation reaches full maturity on the day of the Cross, when the time comes for Mary to receive and beget as her children all those who become disciples, pouring out upon them the saving love of her Son: "When Jesus saw his mother, and the disciple whom he loved standing near, he said to his mother, 'Woman, behold, your son!'" (Jn. 19:26).[16]

Remarkable in its synthesis of the story of Marian Coredemption is John Paul II's General Audience of October

25, 1995, where the essential historical panorama of the development of Marian Coredemption is papally ratified:

> Saying that "the Virgin Mary . . . is acknowledged and honoured as being truly the Mother of God and of the Redeemer" (*Lumen Gentium*, n. 53), the Council draws attention to the link between Mary's motherhood and Redemption.
>
> After becoming aware of the maternal role of Mary, who was venerated in the teaching and worship of the first centuries as the virginal Mother of Jesus Christ and therefore as the Mother of God, in the Middle Ages the Church's piety and theological reflection brought to light her cooperation in the Saviour's work.
>
> This delay is explained by the fact that the efforts of the Church Fathers and of the early Ecumenical Councils, focused as they were on Christ's identity, necessarily left other aspects of dogma aside. Only gradually could the revealed truth be unfolded in all its richness. Down the centuries, Mariology would always take its direction from Christology. The divine motherhood of Mary was itself proclaimed at the Council of Ephesus primarily to affirm the oneness of Christ's person.

Similarly, there was a deeper understanding of Mary's presence in salvation history.

At the end of the second century, St. Irenaeus, a disciple of Polycarp, already pointed out Mary's contribution to the work of salvation. He understood the value of Mary's consent at the time of the Annunciation, recognizing in the Virgin of Nazareth's obedience to and faith in the angel's message the perfect antithesis of Eve's disobedience and disbelief, with a beneficial effect on humanity's destiny. In fact, just as Eve caused death, so Mary, with her "yes," became "a cause of salvation" for herself and for all mankind (cf. *Adv. Haer.*, III, 22, 4; *SC* 211, 441). But this affirmation was not developed in a consistent and systematic way by the other Fathers of the Church.

Instead, this doctrine was systematically worked out for the first time at the end of the 10th century in the *Life of Mary* by a Byzantine monk, John the Geometer. Here Mary is united to Christ in the whole work of Redemption, sharing, according to God's plan, in the Cross and suffering for our salvation. She remained united to the Son "in every deed, attitude and wish" (cf. *Life of Mary*, Bol. 196, f. 123 v.).

> In the West St. Bernard, who died in 1153, turns to Mary and comments on the presentation of Jesus in the temple: "Offer your Son, sacrosanct Virgin, and present the fruit of your womb to the Lord. For our reconciliation with all, offer the heavenly victim pleasing to God" (*Serm. 3 in Purif.*, 2: *PL* 183, 370).
>
> A disciple and friend of St. Bernard, Arnold of Chartres, shed light particularly on Mary's offering in the sacrifice of Calvary. He distinguished in the Cross "two altars: one in Mary's heart, the other in Christ's body. Christ sacrificed his flesh, Mary her soul." Mary sacrificed herself spiritually in deep communion with Christ, and implored the world's salvation: "What the mother asks, the Son approves and the Father grants" (cf. *De septem verbis Domini in cruce*, 3: *PL* 189, 1694).
>
> From this age on other authors explain the doctrine of Mary's special cooperation in the redemptive sacrifice.[17]

The Woman of Calvary is also the Woman of Revelation. In the papal audience of May 29, 1996, the Pope identifies the suffering woman of the Apocalypse as the Mother at the Cross, who suffers to give mystical birth to the community of disciples:

> Identified by her motherhood, the woman "was with child and she cried out in her pangs of birth, in anguish for her delivery" (12:2). This note refers to the Mother of Jesus at the Cross (cf. Jn. 19:25), where she shares in anguish for the delivery of the community of disciples with a soul pierced by the sword (cf. Lk. 2:35). Despite her sufferings, she is "clothed with the sun" — that is, she reflects the divine splendour — and appears as a "great sign" of God's spousal relationship with his people.[18]

In the same address, John Paul reiterates the role of the Immaculate New Eve as the Redeemer's "faithful Collaborator" in her co-operation in the Redemption:

> It was fitting that like Christ, the new Adam, Mary too, the new Eve, did not know sin and was thus capable of co-operating in the Redemption.
>
> Sin, which washes over humanity like a torrent, halts before the Redeemer and his faithful Collaborator. With a substantial difference: Christ is all holy by virtue of the grace that in his humanity derives from the divine person: Mary is all

> holy by virtue of the grace received by the merits of the Saviour.[19]

A landmark catechesis, part of the Pontiff's seventy catechetical teachings on the Blessed Virgin,[20] was delivered on April 2, 1997. During this General Audience, John Paul II puts forth a moving commentary on the Council's teaching on Coredemption and the Mother's compassion at Calvary:

> With our gaze illumined by the radiance of the resurrection, we pause to reflect on the Mother's involvement in her Son's redeeming passion, which was completed by her sharing in his suffering. Let us return again, but now in the perspective of the Resurrection, to the foot of the Cross where the Mother endured "with her only-begotten Son the intensity of his suffering, associated herself with his sacrifice in her mother's heart, and lovingly consented to the immolation of this victim which was born of her."
>
> With these words, the Council reminds us of "Mary's compassion"; in her heart reverberates all that Jesus suffers in body and soul, emphasizing her willingness to share in her Son's redeeming sacrifice and to join her own maternal suffering to

> his priestly offering.
>
> The Council text also stresses that her consent to Jesus' immolation is not passive acceptance but a genuine act of love, by which she offers her Son as a "victim" of expiation for the sins of all humanity.
>
> Lastly, *Lumen Gentium* relates the Blessed Virgin to Christ, who has the lead role in Redemption, making it clear that in associating herself "with his sacrifice" she remains subordinate to her divine Son.[21]

The Holy Father has here penetrated deeply into the compassion of the Mother's Heart at Calvary. "In her heart reverberates all that Jesus suffers in body and soul," and thus she "shares in the redeeming sacrifice." She does not share in the sacrifice formally as "priest," but subordinately as "mother" in a united offering of the one Sacrifice. She offers her Son as "a victim of expiation" for all of humanity's sins.

This catechesis is immediately followed by another inspired instruction on the Mother of God's role as unique "Co-operator" in Redemption on April 9, 1997, which includes the imperative for Christians to participate as "co-redeemers"[22] in the work of distributing the spiritual fruits of Redemption. Only Mary as the Immaculate Co-redemptrix co-operated in the obtaining of graces of Redemption as the New Eve with and under the New Adam on behalf of humanity. The doctrine of Mary Co-redemptrix becomes a crucial "type of the Church" (cf. *Lumen Gentium*, 63), for the People of God are likewise summoned to partake in the mysterious application of Redemption:

> The collaboration of Christians in salvation takes place after the Calvary event, whose fruits they endeavour to spread by prayer and sacrifice. Mary, instead, cooperated during the event itself and in the role of mother; thus her cooperation embraces the whole of Christ's saving work. She alone was associated in this way with the redemptive sacrifice that merited the salvation of all mankind. In union with Christ and in submission to him, she collaborated in obtaining the grace of salvation for all humanity.
>
> The Blessed Virgin's role as cooperator has its source in her divine motherhood. By giving birth to the One who was destined to achieve man's redemption, by nourishing him, presenting him in the temple and suffering with him as he died on the Cross, "in a wholly singular way she cooperated ... in the work of the Saviour" (*Lumen Gentium*, 61). Although God's call to cooperate in the work of salvation concerns every human

> being, the participation of the Saviour's Mother in humanity's Redemption is a unique and unrepeatable fact.[23]

The Mother's meritorious cooperation in man's Redemption originates in her role as "Theotokos" (or "God-bearer"), for she gave birth to the Redeemer and remains "with Jesus" in salvation's work unto the Cross. This is why the Mother of the Redeemer's participation in Redemption is no optional theological speculation, but rather, as the Pontiff declares, a "unique and unrepeatable fact."

Finally, in the Great Year of Jubilee, the Holy Father compares the sacrifice of Mary with the monumental Old Testament sacrifice of Abraham, Father of Faith. But unlike the sacrifice of Abraham, the full execution of the Mother's sacrifice of her Son was demanded of her:

> Daughter of Abraham in faith as well as in the flesh, Mary personally shared in this experience. Like Abraham, she too accepted the sacrifice of her Son, but while the actual sacrifice of Isaac was not demanded of Abraham, Christ drank the cup of suffering to the last drop. Mary personally took part in her Son's trial, believing and hoping at the foot of the Cross (cf. Jn. 19:25).
>
> This was the epilogue of a long wait. Having been taught to meditate on

> the prophetic texts, Mary foresaw what awaited her and in praising the mercy of God, faithful to his people from generation to generation, she gave her own consent to his plan of salvation; in particular, she said her "yes" to the central event of this plan, the sacrifice of that Child whom she bore in her womb. Like Abraham, she accepted the sacrifice of her Son.[24]

John Paul's courageous testimony to Mary Co-redemptrix perseveres indefinitely, meriting for him the singular title of "Pope of the Co-redemptrix." As the length of days of his pontificate continue to surprise and to feed the world, so too does his ongoing homage to the Mother of the Redeemer. His papal and filial tribute to Mary Co-redemptrix will continue until his papacy and life come to its providential closure.

Notes

[1] For a more extended treatment, cf. Calkins, "Pope John Paul II's Teaching on Marian Coredemption," pp. 113-147; also "The Mystery of Mary Coredemptrix in the Papal Magisterium," *Mary Co-redemptrix: Doctrinal Issue Today*, pp. 41-47.

[2] John Paul II, *Insegnamenti di Giovanni Paolo II*, Libreria Editrice Vaticana, 1978-, V/3, 1982, 404.

[3] John Paul II, *L'Osservatore Romano*, English edition, November 12, 1984, p. 1.

[4] *Ibid.*, March 11, 1985, p. 7.

[5] Unfortunately, these were the expressions used to describe the significance of the repeated papal usages of the title of Co-redemptrix by Pope John Paul II, as contained in an unsigned article which appeared in *L'Osservatore Romano* on June 4, 1997. This article accompanied the brief conclusion of an ad hoc ecumenical committee of theologians (sixteen Catholic and five non-Catholic), who met at the 1996 Czestochowa Marian Conference to study the possibility of a dogmatic definition of Mary as Co-redemptrix, Mediatrix of all graces, and Advocate (a meeting estimated by the committee members to have lasted less than one hour).

Although the ad hoc committee members later stated that they were not informed that they were in any way acting as an official "papal commission," their conclusions were nonetheless published some ten months later in *L'Osservatore Romano* as the conclusions of a "commission established by the Holy See" and released as a "Declaration of the Theological Commission of the Congress of the Pontifical International Marian Academy" (*L'Osservatore Romano*, June 4, 1997). This publication happened to immediately follow a meeting of some seventy bishops and one hundred theologians and international lay leaders at the Domus Mariae Conference Center in Rome (members of the international Marian movement, *Vox Populi Mariae Mediatrici*), who presented the Holy Father with a votum for the papal definition of Mary as Co-redemptrix, Mediatrix of all graces and Advocate, based in part upon the theological foundations of the papal teachings of Pope John Paul II, and containing the petitions of over five-hundred-fifty bishops, including forty-five cardinals, and over six million petitions from the Catholic laity worldwide.

The commission's statement was published while the Holy Father was on a pastoral visit to Poland. On several points, the conclusions of the commission directly contradict the Pope's own teaching and practice regarding Marian Coredemption and the legitimate use of the title of Co-redemptrix. For an extended treatment, cf. M. Miravalle, *In Continued Dialogue With the Czestochowa Commission*, Queenship, 2002.

[6] John Paul II, *L'Osservatore Romano*, English edition, April 9, 1985, p. 12.

[7] John Paul II, *Inseg.*, XIII/1, 1990, 743:1.

[8] John Paul II, *L'Osservatore Romano*, English edition, October 14, 1991, p. 4.

[9] *Ibid.*, May 9, 1983, p. 1

[10] *Ibid.*, June 13, 1983, p. 2.

[11] *Ibid.*, December 12, 1983, p. 1.

[12] John Paul II, Apostolic Letter *Salvifici Doloris*, 25.

[13] Classic terminology in expressing this participation in the acquisition of redemptive graces of Calvary include "Redemption *in actu primo*" or participation in "objective Redemption."

[14] Pius XI, *L'Osservatore Romano*, December 1, 1933, p. 1.

[15] John Paul II, *L'Osservatore Romano*, English edition, September 16, 1991, p. 4.

[16] John Paul II, Encyclical *Evangelium Vitae*, March 25, 1995, 103; *AAS* 87, 1995, p. 520.

[17] John Paul II, *L'Osservatore Romano*, English edition, November 1, 1995, p. 11.

[18] *Ibid.*, June 5, 1996, p. 11

[19] *Ibid.*

[20] From September 1995 to November 1997, John Paul II offered

seventy Catechetical teachings of the Blessed Virgin Mary, which have been assembled and published under the title *Theotókos: Woman, Mother, Disciple: A Catechesis on Mary, Mother of God*, Pauline Books and Media, 2000.

[21] John Paul II, *L'Osservatore Romano*, English edition, April 9, 1997, p. 7.

[22] On at least three occasions, John Paul has underscored the call for Christians to become "co-redeemers" in the distribution of the graces of Calvary obtained by Jesus and Mary, and for Christians to participate in "coredemption." Due to its importance to Mary Co-redemptrix as an authentic model for the Church, we here include the direct references: "Is it necessary to remind all of you, sorely tried by suffering, who are listening to me, that your pain unites you more and more with the Lamb of God, who 'takes away the sin of the world' through his Passion (Jn. 1:29)? And that therefore you, too, associated with him in suffering, can be coredeemers of mankind? You know these shining truths. Never tire of offering your sufferings for the Church, that all her children may be consistent with their faith, persevering in prayer and fervent in hope" (addressing the sick at the Hospital of the Brothers of St. John of God (Fatebenefratelli) on Rome's Tiber Island on April 5, 1981, *L'Osservatore Romano*, English edition, April 13, 1981, p. 6); "To the sick who are present and to those who are in hospital wards, in nursing homes and in families I say: never feel alone, because the Lord is with you and will never abandon you. Be courageous and strong: unite your pains and sufferings to those of the Crucified and you will become coredeemers of humanity, together with Christ" (spoken while addressing the sick after a general audience given January 13, 1982, *Inseg.*, V/1, 1982, 91); "'The candidate should be irreproachable' (Tit. 1:6), Saint Paul admonishes again. Personal spiritual direction should cultivate in them [candidates for the priesthood] an unlimited love for Christ and his Mother, and a great desire to unite themselves closely to the work of coredemption" (addressing the Bishops of Uruguay gathered in Montevideo concerning candidates for the priesthood,

May 8, 1988, *L'Osservatore Romano*, English edition, May 30, 1988, p. 4).

[23] John Paul II, *L'Osservatore Romano*, English edition, April 16, 1997, p. 7.

[24] *Ibid.*, March 1, 2000, p. 11.

Chapter XIV

Contemporary Saints and Mary Co-redemptrix

The mind of a saint is supernaturally disposed to the truth. The more sanctified the human heart, the more docile is the human mind to revealed mysteries of faith. The saints have sacrificed all worldly desires for sake of the heavenly paradise, and therefore have much less propensity for their intellects being skewed or confused due to attachments of the world — human agenda, ecclesiastical or otherwise, which can obscure divine truths and impede their assent.

The testimony of the saints and blesseds represents the highest, most trustworthy level of *sensus fidelium* — that common consensus of Christian faith found within the People of God, which is in its own way inspired and protected by the Spirit of Truth.[1]

The "voice of the people" (*vox populi*), according to the ancient Church maxim, is an echo of the "voice of God" (*vox Dei*). Among this *vox populi* chorus, the witness of the saints offers the most pure and genuine refrain in recognizing, living, and sometimes dying for Christian truth. It is therefore particularly valuable to listen to their songs in praise of Mary Co-redemptrix.

We are keenly aware of the limitations of our treatment of the illustrious and expansive testimony by God's saints to their *Mater Dolorosa.* We restrict ourselves here to the most recent testimonies, in fact, only those saints and blesseds who have died within the last hundred years. This genus is itself radically limited to those who have been canonized or beatified within one hundred years of death.

St. Gemma Galgani († 1903) was an Italian saint who in her short twenty-five years of life experienced many supernatural manifestations, including visions of Jesus, diabolical attacks, and the stigmata. During some of her recorded ecstasies, St. Gemma speaks powerfully of the Mother's coredemptive sufferings at Calvary:

> Oh wicked sinners, stop crucifying Jesus, because at the same time you are also transfixing the Mother .... Oh my Mother, where do I find you? Always at the foot of the Cross of Jesus . . . Oh what pain was yours! . . . I no longer see one sacrifice only, I see two of them: one for Jesus, one for Mary! . . . Oh my Mother, if one were to see you with Jesus he would not be able to say who is the first to expire: is it you or Jesus? [2]
>
> What compassion you show me, oh my Mother, to see you so every Saturday

> at the foot of the Cross! . . . Oh! I no longer see one Victim only, but there are two.[3]

St. Gemma writes to her spiritual director of the sufferings of the Blessed Virgin from the time of Jesus' birth onward as she painfully pondered his Crucifixion:

> Oh what great sorrow it must have been for the Mother, after Jesus was born, to think that they had then to crucify Him! What pangs she must have always had in her Heart! How many sighs she must have made, and how many times she must have wept! Yet she never complained. Poor Mother![4]
>
> . . . truly, then, when she sees Him being crucified . . . that poor Mother was transfixed by many arrows . . . Therefore my Mother was crucified together with Jesus.[5]

We have previously discussed the ecclesiastical approval of Mary Co-redemptrix which took place under the pontificate of Pope St. Pius X († 1914).[6] During his pontificate, three documents of the Roman Curia refer to the "merciful Co-redemptrix of the human race," "our Co-redemptrix" and "Co-redemptrix of the human race."[7] In his own words, the canonized Pope instructs in his 1904 Marian encyclical, *Ad Diem Illum* of the "communion of life and sorrows between Mother and Son" in her offering of the redemptive victim: "[Mary would have] the task of guarding and nourishing the Victim, and of placing Him on the altar. From this is derived that communion of life and of sorrows between Mother and Son, sorrows to which, for both of them in equal manner, can be applied the words of the Prophet: 'My life is consumed in sorrow, my years are passed in groaning' (Ps. 30: 1)."[8]

St. Pius X moreover invokes our Immaculate Mother as the "Reparatrix of the lost world" and therefore the "Dispensatrix of all the treasures which Jesus merited for us with his bloody death."[9] He also quotes St. Bonaventure in speaking of the depth of the Mother's redemptive participation at Calvary, stating that Mary "so participated in the [Son's] suffering that, if it were possible, she would have been most happy to suffer herself all the torments which were supported by the Son."[10]

St. Francis Xavier Cabrini († 1917), the first American citizen to be canonized, gives repeated laud to the Co-redemptrix in her teachings and sayings.[11] She calls the Blessed Virgin the "New Eve, true Mother of the Living" who was "chosen by God to become the Co-redemptrix of the human race."[12] Mother Cabrini also elaborates upon the coredemptive papal teachings of her contemporary, St. Pius X, in this commentary on the Co-redemptrix:

> If the glory of giving life to our Redeemer pertained to her, then also, as our Holy Father said so well, the office of guarding

> and preparing the Sacred Victim of the human race for sacrifice pertained to her as well. Mary was not only the Mother of Jesus in the joys of Bethlehem, but even more so on Calvary, . . . and there she merited to become our most worthy Co-redemptrix.[13]

St. Maximilian Maria Kolbe († 1941) is the "Immaculata's theologian" and therefore he is also theologian of the Co-redemptrix. The Polish martyr-saint who himself heroically lived the mystery of Coredemption by offering his life in exchange for another prisoner at Auschwitz, offers exceptional tribute to the Co-redemptrix as the predestined partner with the predestined Redeemer in restoring grace to mankind: "From that moment [of the Fall] God promised a Redeemer and a Co-redemptrix saying: 'I will place enmities between thee and the Woman, and thy seed and her Seed; She shall crush thy head.'"[14] St. Maximilian goes on to encourage the more complete understanding of Mary Co-redemptrix for our contemporary times: "Clearly, our relationship with Mary Co-redemptrix and Dispensatrix of graces in the economy of Redemption was not understood from the beginning in all its perfection. But in these, our times, faith in the Blessed Virgin Mary's mediation continues to grow more and more each day."[15]

This wisdom concerning the maturity of doctrinal development of Co-redemptrix as an essential part of her universal mediation led St. Maximilian to be one of the first, along with the renowned Belgian Cardinal Mercier, to encourage the solemn papal definition of Our Lady's mediation in 1923. Aware of the intentions of Pope Benedict XV to establish three theological commissions to study the question of the definability of Mary's universal mediation,[16] St. Maximilian calls for prayers to Our Mother to hasten its solemn proclamation, since Our Lady's role as the Mediatrix of all graces constitutes the underlying theological basis for the act of Marian consecration and for the activities of his *Militia Immaculatae* ("Army of the Immaculate"):

> Cardinal Mercier says: "With the briefing of November 28, 1922, the Holy Father told us of his decision to nominate three delegations: one in Rome, another in Spain and the third in Belgium. They were to examine in detail the following problem: does the mediation of the Most Blessed Virgin Mary belong to the revealed truths, and can it be a matter of definition?"
>
> . . . On this truth the Militia bases its activities. We have recourse to the Immaculata and we are instruments in Her hands, because She distributes all the graces of conversion and sanctification to the inhabitants of this valley of tears. Furthermore, we clearly profess this truth in our act of consecration to the Virgin Mary because every grace passes through Her hands from the Sweetest Heart of the

> pure Jesus to us. But on what basis? Let us look at history. All conversions have always come through Mary, and every saint had a particular devotion to her. The Fathers and the Doctors of the Church have proclaimed that She, the second Eve, has repaired what the first destroyed: that She is the channel of all graces, that She is our hope and refuge, that we receive our graces through her. In his encyclical on the Rosary (Sept. 22, 1891), Pope Leo XIII says: "It can be affirmed in all truth that according to the divine will nothing of the immense treasury of grace can be communicated to us except through Mary." Let us pray, therefore, that our Holy Mother may expedite the solemn proclamation of this Her privilege, so that all humanity may run to Her feet with complete trust, since today we are in great need of Her protection.[17]

The Co-redemptrix and Ecumenism

St. Leopold Mandic († 1942), a Croatian Capuchin priest stationed in Padua, was an internationally celebrated confessor and spiritual director for almost forty years. Physically weak, suffering from numerous difficulties of body and speech due to several illnesses, he was a spiritual giant who spent twelve hours a day in the confessional as an ordained "channel of reconciliation." An apostle and "victim for ecumenism," St. Leopold offered his life to the Co-redemptrix for the re-unification of the Oriental Churches with the Church of Rome. So extraordinarily dedicated was this saint to Mary Co-redemptrix that he had a lifelong desire to author a book in defense of the Blessed Mother as "Co-redemptrix of the human race," and the "channel of every grace" that comes from Jesus Christ.[18]

St. Leopold refers to the Mother as "Co-redemptrix of the human race" no less than thirteen times, and also rekindles the medieval and modern title of "our Redemptrix."[19] So stouthearted a defender of the Co-redemptrix was Leopold, that above one of his images he once wrote the following personal testimony: "I, friar Leopold Mandic Zarevic, firmly believe that the most Blessed Virgin, insofar as she was Co-redemptrix of the human race, is the moral fountain of all grace, since we have received all from her fullness."[20]

To convey the unconditional nature of dedication to the Co-redemptrix lived by this Patron of Church reunification, St. Leopold writes this oath of victimhood in his own hand, wherein he offers his entire life "in submission to the Co-redemptrix of the human race" for the "redemption" and reconciliation of the Oriental peoples: "In truth, before God and the Blessed Virgin, confirming all by oath, I myself am obliged, in submission to the Co-redemptrix of the human race, to exert all my life's strength, in accord with the obedience I owe my superiors, for the redemption of all dissident Oriental peoples from schism and error."[21]

The human witness of St. Leopold to both the undeniable truth of Mary Co-redemptrix and the authentic imperative of Christian ecumenism provides concrete proof in a canonized human life that generous Church devotion to Mary Co-redemptrix in no way opposes authentic Catholic ecumenical activity. In fact, the "Minister of reconciliation"[22] shows us that the Co-redemptrix is the Marian means for true Christian reconciliation as "our Common Mother,"[23] to use the expression of John Paul II. Thus, the Mother Co-redemptrix is also the Mother of the Ecumenical Movement, and never its obstacle.

Along with the example of St. Leopold, we have the current example of John Paul II, who is both "fully Marian and fully ecumenical." He is Pope of the Co-redemptrix without violating the true meaning or imperative of Christian ecumenism. For the ecumenical mission of the Church consists of prayer as its "soul" and dialogue as its "body" in seeking true Christian unity with the one, holy, catholic, and apostolic Church of Jesus Christ.[24] In his encyclical on ecumenism, *Ut Unum Sint*, the Holy Father forbids all doctrinal compromise in efforts to achieve this goal: "In the Body of Christ, 'the way, the truth, and the life' (Jn. 14:6), who could consider legitimate a reconciliation brought about at the expense of truth?"[25]

Therefore, it is not an authentic Catholic option to believe "either" in Mary Co-redemptrix or in ecumenism, but rather *a duty and obligation to believe in both.* For it is precisely through the role of Mary Co-redemptrix that the reunion of Christians will occur.

The acclaimed philosopher, convert and cloistered Carmelite nun, St. Teresa Benedicta of the Cross († 1942) has been proclaimed the "co-Patroness of Europe." Born of a Jewish family as Edith Stein, St. Teresa Benedicta was another victim of Auschwitz. Before the final offering of her life she gave the world her philosophically personalist insights and her mystical meditations.

Deeply devoted to Our Lady of Sorrows, St. Teresa Benedicta spent numerous hours of prayer before the image of the Sorrowful Mother, and described the Mother Co-redemptrix as our entry into the "redemptive order."[26] Like her Heavenly Mother, she was first an "illustrious daughter of Israel"[27] before becoming a disciple of Christ.

In her theological treatise, *Scientia Crucis*, in which she discusses the knowledge of the Cross according to St. John of the Cross, St. Teresa Benedicta confirms with Dionysius that the human person's greatest act is to co-operate with God in human salvation: "The divinest of all divine work is to co-operate with God in the salvation of souls."[28] But it is Our Lady who co-operates in this divine work beyond all creatures. St. Teresa Benedicta states in a truly pregnant line that the role of the Co-redemptrix transcends the merely human level of activity and enters the supernatural realm of human co-operation: "Mary leaves the natural order and is placed as Co-redemptrix alongside the Redeemer."[29]

The humble Mary of Nazareth departs from the natural order of being as a daughter of Adam and Eve, and accepts her predestination by God to become the spiritual Mother of all peoples. She does this by being "placed alongside the Redeemer" in the supernatural order, the hypostatic order, the universally redemptive order. She is the spiritual Mother of all peoples through her co-operation with God for the salvation of souls, the "divinest of divine works." The Jewish-born Carmelite and Co-Patroness of Europe further reveres the ultimate Daughter Zion as the "Collaboratrix of Christ the Redeemer."[30]

Opus Dei Founder, St. Jose Maria Escrivà († 1975) was an exceptional modern apostle who perennially encouraged the members of the worldwide "Work of God" to appreciate their Heavenly Mother in all her salvific roles. St. Jose Maria vigorously defends our Lady as the Co-redemptrix in this passage where he applauds the papal usage of the Co-redemptrix title and its doctrine:

> The Supreme Pontiffs have rightly called Mary 'Co-redemptrix.' At that point, together with her Son who was suffering and dying, she suffered and almost died; at that point she abdicated her maternal rights over her Son for the salvation of humanity and immolated Him, insofar as she was able, in order to placate the justice of God; thus one can rightly say that she redeemed the human race together with Christ. In this fashion we are in a better position to

> understand that moment of the Lord's Passion which we should never grow tired of meditating upon: 'Stabat iuxta crucem Jesus Mater eius,' 'Now there stood by the Cross of Jesus His Mother' (Jn. 19:25).[31]

Regarding the historic saint-stigmatist, St. Pio of Pietrelcina († 1968), truly no introduction is necessary, nor would one be adequate.

Padre Pio's consecration and oblation to the Coredemptive Madonna was boundless within the confines of hyperdulia. The mystical saint of the confessional would constantly direct his penitents to the Mother of Sorrows and perennially gave them the sacramental penance of reciting seven Hail Mary's to the Lady of Sorrows; several penitents report that before he could fully announce this Marian title he would often break into tears.[32]

His perpetual accolade to the Mother of Sorrows and Co-redemptrix contained within his myriad counsels in the confessional and his daily spiritual advice can be summarized by a written testimony to the Co-redemptrix from one of his letters: "Now I seem to be penetrating what was the martyrdom of our most beloved Mother . . . . Oh, if all people would but penetrate this martyrdom! Who could succeed in suffering with this, yes, our dear Coredemptrix? Who would refuse her the good title of Queen of Martyrs?"[33]

The Blesseds

A number of contemporary Blesseds join their voices to the saints who praise Mary Co-redemptrix.

Blessed Bartolo Longo († 1926) has recently been the object of renewed veneration, due to John Paul II's prominent quoting of the "Apostle of the Rosary" in his 2002 Apostolic Letter on the Rosary, *Rosarium Virginis Mariae*.[34] Our Lady is "all-powerful by grace" professes Blessed Bartolo, and he repeatedly invokes the Immaculate One as "our Co-redemptrix and Dispensatrix of Graces."[35] His heartfelt invocation to the Co-redemptrix for his times should likewise become our own prayerful petition for ours: "O Holy Virgin, fulfill today your office of being our Co-redemptrix."[36]

Religious founder and protégé of St. John Bosco, Blessed Luigi Orione († 1940) utilizes the Co-redemptrix title: "Mary is Co-redemptrix of humanity; she is our most tender Mother because she even wept, especially for this reason . . . ."[37]

The great Marian Cardinal of Milan, Blessed Idlephonse Cardinal Schuster († 1954) promulgates an authoritative Mariology of Mary Co-redemptrix with generous usages of the Co-redemptrix title throughout his prolific theological writings, homilies, and catechetical works.[38]

The cardinal-theologian presents an elaborate Mariology of the Co-redemptrix: "Even in Heaven Mary exercises the office of being our Advocate, that office which

Jesus entrusted to her on Calvary; this is so that the Redemption might completely repair the fall, even in superabundance. To Adam and Eve, sinners and the source of original sin in this world, God has countered with Christ and Mary, the Redeemer and Coredemptrix of the human race."[39] Regarding the Feast of Our Lady of Sorrows, he writes:

> The special devotion to the Sorrows of the Virgin, Coredemptrix of the human race, was already within the soul of the Christian people many centuries ago ... [The modern September 15 Feast, however, was] rather the feast of the triumph of the Blessed Mother who, at the foot of the Cross, precisely by means of her cruel martyrdom, redeemed the human race together with her Son, and merited the triumph of her exaltation above all the choirs of Angels and Saints.[40]

In his commentary of the Presentation, Blessed Idlephonse says of the elderly Simeon that he "already discerns from afar the Cross planted on Calvary, and he foresees Mary Coredemptrix at the foot of the Cross with her Heart transfixed by the sword . . . Mary heard the old man, understood, but did not utter a word. Her unbloody martyrdom began from that moment, but she kept silence, because the victim usually keeps quiet and does not speak."[41]

Blessed James Alberione († 1971), a modern apostle of social communications and evangelization, is Founder of the Pious Society of St. Paul, which has disseminated Catholic books and media resources to the four corners of the earth. His extensive Mariology of Coredemption is theologically astute while at the same time appealing to the Christian heart:

> As Jesus in the Garden of Gethsemani agreed to offer Himself, so too Mary gave her consent to the immolation and, insofar as it stood within her power, she immolated her Son. Her consent was in a different mode, but similar to that given for the Incarnation . . . And the union of wills and intentions and sorrows between Mother and Son never came to be interrupted throughout Their lives; and much less was that union broken on Calvary . . . As a result of that union of sorrows, wills and intentions between Mary and Jesus Christ, Mary became Reparatrix and our Coredemptrix and the Dispensatrix of the fruits of the Cross . . . The Redeemer is Jesus alone. Jesus is the principal Mediator by office; Mary is the secondary and associated Redemptrix to this great work by the divine will.[42]

With succinct theological precision, Blessed Alberione explains the Mother's lifelong coredemptive mission: "[She] suffered in union with Jesus the Redeemer; she was Coredemptrix. She knew that this was her mission, to give worthy satisfaction for sin, to reopen Heaven, to save mankind. She fulfilled this, her office, from Jesus' crib even to Calvary, and to Jesus' Sepulcher."[43] With the same precision, he identifies Mary's role in grace acquisition and its result in grace distribution: "[Mary] cooperated in the acquisition of grace, and therefore she is Coredemptrix; she exposes our needs to God, and therefore she is Mediatrix of grace; she loves us and communicates the divine mercy to us, and therefore she is our spiritual Mother."[44]

From the company of recent Venerables, we cite the eminent scripture scholar and missionary to China, Venerable Gabriel Mary Allegra († 1974). Venerable Gabriel staunchly defended the dogmatic definability of Mary as Co-redemptrix and Mediatrix of all graces, particularly on its biblical foundations:[45] "I firmly believe and with all my strength I will preach to the rest of the faithful that the title of Coredemptrix is theologically exact in explaining the part that Mary had in the work of our salvation."[46] This eminently respected scripture scholar tells us: "The afflictions of Mary and those of Jesus were but one affliction which made two Hearts to suffer . . . The Compassion of Mary increased the suffering of Jesus and the Passion of Jesus was the source of Mary's sorrows. This double offering redeemed the world."[47] Venerable Allegra furthermore notes that "Mary merited the title, Co-redemptrix"[48] and that "she intimately united herself to her dying Son on the Cross as our Co-redemptrix."[49]

We end this unified song of praise from the Christian elect with the solo voice of the recently beatified Mother Teresa of Calcutta († 1997), whose Mariological profundity-in-simplicity resound in a 1993 letter of support for the dogmatic definition of Mary Co-redemptrix:

14, August 1993
Feast of St. Maximilian Kolbe

> Mary is our Coredemptrix with Jesus. She gave Jesus his body and suffered with him at the foot of the cross.
>
> Mary is the Mediatrix of all grace. She gave Jesus to us, and as our Mother she obtains for us all his graces.
>
> Mary is our Advocate who prays to Jesus for us. It is only through the Heart of Mary that we come to the Eucharistic Heart of Jesus.
>
> The papal definition of Mary as Coredemptrix, Mediatrix, and Advocate will bring great graces to the Church.
>
> All for Jesus through Mary.

God bless you
M. Teresa, M.C. [50]

Notes

[1] Cf. M. de Maria, "Il 'sensus fidei' e la 'Corredentrice,'" *Maria Corredentrice*, Frigento, 2000, vol. 3, p. 8. For extended treatments, cf. S. M. Miotto, "La voce dei Santi e la 'Corredentrice,'" *Maria Corredentrice*, pp. 189-223; S. Manelli, F.F.I., "Marian Coredemption in the Hagiography of the 20th Century," *Mary Co-redemptrix: Doctrinal Issues Today*, pp. 191-261; Note: The majority of references contained in this chapter can be found in these two more comprehensive works.

[2] St. Gemma Galgani, *Estasi, Diario, Autobiografica, Scritti vari*, Rome, 1988, p. 24.

[3] *Ibid.*, p. 34.

[4] St. Gemma Galgani, *Lettere*, Rome, 1979, p. 106.

[5] *Ibid.*

[6] Cf. Chapter XI.

[7] Cf. *ASS* 41, 1908, p. 409; *AAS* 5, 1913, p. 364; *AAS* 6, 1914, p. 108.

[8] St. Pius X, *Ad Diem Illum*, 12.

[9] *Ibid.*

[10] *Ibid.*

[11] Cf. G. de Luca, *Parole sparse della Beata Cabrini*, Rome, 1938.

[12] *Ibid.*, p. 164, 169.

[13] *Ibid.*, p. 170.

[14] St. Maximilian Kolbe, *Scritti*, Rome, 1997, n. 1069. Also cf. L. Iammorrone, "Il mistero di Maria Corredentrice in san Massimiliano Kolbe," *Maria Corredentrice*, vol. 2, pp. 219-256; H. M. Manteau-Bonamy, O.P., *Immaculate Conception and the Holy Spirit*, pp. 99-102.

[15] St. Maximilian Kolbe, *Scritti*, n. 1229.

[16] Both Spanish and Belgian commissions strongly recommended the solemn definition of Mary's universal mediation; the Roman commission's conclusions were never officially published, cf. M. O'Carroll, C.S.Sp., "The Fifth Marian Dogma and the Commission: Theological Gaps," *Contemporary Insights on a Fifth Marian Dogma*, p. 143.

[17] St. Maximilian Kolbe, "The Mediation of the Most Blessed Virgin Mary," *Rycerz Niepokalanej,* 1923, vol. 3, pp. 45-46.

[18] Cf. P. E. Bernardi, *Leopoldo Mandic: Santo della riconciliazione*, Padua, 1990, p. 118.

[19] Cf. P. Tieto, *Suo umile servo in Cristo*, vol. 2, *Scritti*, Padua, 1992, p. 117. Also for an extended treatment, cf. P. Stemman, "Il mistero di Maria 'Corredentrice' nella vita e negli Insegnamenti di san Leopoldo Mandic," *Maria Corredentrice*, Frigento, 1999, vol. 2, pp. 257-276.

[20] St. Leopold Mandic, *Scritti*, vol. 2, p. 124.

[21] Cf. Stemman, "Il mistero di Maria 'Corredentrice,'" p. 269. The original Latin text is as follows: "Vere coram Deo et Deiparae Virgini, interposita sacramenti fide, me obstrinxi in obsequium Corredemptricis humani generis, disponendi omnes ratione vitae meae iuxta oboedientiam meorum superiorum in redemptionem Orientalium Dissidentium a schismate et errore." St. Leopold Mandic, *Scritti*, vol. 2, p. 97.

[22] Cf. Stemman, "Il mistero di Maria 'Corredentrice,'" p. 262.

[23] John Paul II, *Redemptoris Mater*, 30

[24] Cf. John Paul II, Encyclical *Ut Unum Sint*, 21, 28.

[25] *Ut Unum Sint*, 18.

[26] Cf. F. Oben, *Edith Stein*, Alba House, 1988, pp. 57-61, 67.

[27] Pope John Paul II, Beatification Discourse in Cologne, May 1, 1987.

[28] Edith Stein, *The Science of the Cross: A Study of St. John of the Cross*, eds. Dr. Lucy Gelber and Fr. Romaeus Leuven, O.C.D., trans. Hilda C. Graef, Henry Regnery Co., 1960, p. 215.

[29] *Ibid*. Cf. also Sr. M. F. Perella, "Edith Stein. Ebrea, carmelitana, martire," *Palestra del Clero*, 1999, vol. 78, p. 695. Note: A contemporaneous author from the Rhineland countries is the Swiss mystic and stigmatist, Adrienne von Speyr († 1967), who was a close associate of the Swiss theologian, Hans Urs von Balthasar. The inseparability of thought between von Balthasar and von Speyr is confirmed by von Balthasar himself: "I want to try to prevent anyone after my death from undertaking the task of separating my

work from that of Adrienne von Speyr. This is not in the least possible" (Hans Urs von Balthasar, *Unser Auftrag*, 11). The recipient of hundreds of revelations during her lifetime, von Speyr puts forth an outstanding theological and mystical account of the Mother Co-redemptrix. In her book, *Mary in the Redemption* (Ignatius Press, 2003), she uses the title ten times throughout the work amidst penetrating theological insights. For example: " . . . And Mary is so loyal to the Father that in her own Son she sees both the one who has been appointed by the Father (for she is always one with the Father's will) and increasingly, through the Son, the Father himself. However, it will be much harder for the Son to take her, the innocent, with him into his Passion and to make use of her purity in a way that involves her in the work of redemption and makes her Co-redemptrix. It will be much harder to involve one who is immaculate in all this than a convert, who has many personal things for which to atone and therefore gladly cooperates in bearing a share of the common guilt. The sacrificing of the Mother here approaches the killing of the 'innocents'" (*Mary in the Redemption*, p. 32).

And also from von Speyr: " . . . Since the Son chose her as his Mother, she will remain his Mother even in his death. He has chosen her for everything, and her co-redemption was already planned and contained in her pre-redemption. She was, therefore, Co-redemptrix when she gave birth to him. Her giving birth was an act dedicated to the Son so that he might fulfill his mission, an act whose meaning is contained in his divine-human mission. And this meaning is not lost on Mary. She remains his Mother whether he is in her, whether he has gone forth from her, or whether he hangs on the Cross" (*Mary in the Redemption*, p. 83-84).

[30] St. Teresa Benedicta, *Beata Teresa Benedetta della Croce, Vita Dottrina, Testi inediti*, Rome, 1997, p. 1997

[31] St. Jose Maria Escrivà, *Amici di Dio. Omelie*, Milan, 1978, p. 318; also cf. Miotto, "La voce dei Santi e la 'Corredentrice,'" p. 215; F. Delelaux, "Nel dolore invocare e imitare Maria Corredentrice," *Eco del Santuario dell'Addolorata*, Castelpetroso, 1995, n. 3, pp. 6-8, n. 4, pp. 3-5.

[32] A. Negrisolo, N. Castello, S. M. Manelli, *Padre Pio nella sua interiorità*, Rome, 1997, pp. 123.

[33] St. Padre Pio, *Epistolario*, San Giovanni Rotondo, 1992, vol. 3, p. 384; cf. also these works on Padre Pio: Castello, Manelli, *La "dolce Signora" di Padre Pio*, Cinisello Balsamo, IT 1999; Manelli, "Maria SS.ma Corredentrice nella vita e negli scritti di Padre Pio da Pietrelcina," *Maria Corredentrice*, Frigento, vol. 2, pp. 277-294; M. Da Pobladura, *Alla scuola spirituale di Padre Pio da Pietrelcina*, San Giovanni Rotondo, 1978; F. Da Riese, *P. Pio da Pietrelcina crocifisso senza croce*, Foggia, 1991.

[34] John Paul II, Apostolic Letter *Rosarium Virginis Mariae*, October 16, 2002, 43.

[35] Bl. Bartolo Longo, *I quindici sabati del santo Rosario*, Pompeii, 1996 ed., p. 62; English trans., *The Fifteen Saturdays*, Pompeii, 1993, p. 65.

[36] Bl. Bartolo Longo, *I quindici sabati*, pp. 98, 101.

[37] Bl. Luigi Orione, cited in anthology *Con don Orione verso Maria*, Rome, 1987, p. 215; cf. also Miotto, "La voce dei Santi e la 'Corredentrice.'"

[38] Cf. I. Schuster, *Liber Sacramentorum. Note storiche e liturgiche sul Messale Romano*, Turin-Rome, 1928, vol. 9; *L'Evangelo di Nostra Donna*, Milan, 1954.

[39] *Ibid.*, vol. 8, p.181.

[40] *Ibid.*, vol. 7, p. 89.

[41] Schuster, *L'Evangelo di Nostra Donna*, Milan, p. 67.

[42] G. Alberione, *Maria Regina degli Apostoli*, Rome, 1948, pp. 110-111; cf. also Manelli, "Maria Corredentrice nel pensiero del venerabile Giacomo Alberione," *Maria Corredentrice*, Frigento, 2000, pp. 163-188.

[43] Alberione, *Brevi meditazioni per ogni giorno dell'anno*, Rome, 1952, vol. 1, pp. 452-453.

[44] Alberione, *Le grandezze di Maria Feste di Maria Santissima*, Albano, 1954, p. 42.

[45] Cf. Murabito, "La Corredenzione di Maria nel pensiero del venerabile Padre Gabriele Allegra," *Maria Corredentrice*, Frigento, 1999, vol. 2, pp. 195-314.

[46] G. M. Allegra, *Fasciculus Florum*, Quaderno, Nov. 18, 1939; *Archivio della Vice Postulazione.*

[47] Allegra, *I sette dolori di Maria*, Castelpetroso, 1995, pp. 30-31.

[48] *Ibid.*, p. 30.

[49] Allegra, *Il Cuore Immacolato di Maria*, Acireale, 1991, p. 132.

[50] Blessed Teresa of Calcutta, *Letter to Vox Populi Mariae Mediatrici*, Aug. 14, 1993, *Vox Populi Mariae Mediatrici* Archives, Hopedale, Ohio.

Chapter XV

Fatima and Mary Co-redemptrix

In the Church-approved messages of Our Lady of the Rosary at Fatima, Portugal (1917), the Woman clothed with the sun exhorts the young visionaries and the world to "sacrifice yourselves for sinners"[1] and "to make of everything you can a sacrifice and offer it to God as an act of reparation for the sins by which He is offended."[2] It is a call for human coredemption, exemplified by its Queen.

Our Lady invites Lucia, Jacinta, and Francisco to a life of coredemption for the salvation of souls: "Are you willing to offer yourselves to God and bear all the suffering He wills to send you, as an act of reparation for the conversion of sinners?"[3] The children faithfully respond to this heavenly invitation to be co-redeemers, "Yes, we are willing." The Co-redemptrix in turn responds, "Then you are going to have much to suffer, but the grace of God will be your comfort."[4] It was precisely their heroic fiat to the Fatima call of human coredemption that led to the beatification of Jacinta and Francisco by John Paul II on May 13, 2002. [5]

In the monumental apparition of July 13, 1917, which predicts great upcoming trials and persecutions for the Church and world, and specifically for the Holy Father,[6] Our Lady of Fatima again directs the children to "sacrifice yourselves for sinners" and identifies her own coredemptive mediation and the consistent praying of the Holy Rosary as the only true remedy by which to obtain peace in the world: ". . . Continue to pray the Rosary every day in honor of Our Lady of the Rosary, in order to obtain peace in the world and the ending of the war, because only she can help you."[7] It is thereby most fitting that she would later appear on October 13 during the historic event of the great solar miracle under the appearance of Our Lady of Sorrows.[8]

Indeed human coredemption envelops the July 13 Fatima message, with its call for Christian offering of sacrifice and consecration to the Immaculate Heart of Mary. In addition, Our Lady of the Rosary predicts an eventual *Triumph of the Immaculate Heart of Mary* as the fruit of various levels of human cooperation: "In the end, my Immaculate Heart will triumph."[9]

A recent book authored by Sr. Lucia, the remaining visionary still alive, undeniably identifies the doctrine of Mary Co-redemptrix as being at the very heart of the Fatima message. In her 1998 work, *Calls from the Message of Fatima*, she provides an inspired theological and mystical witness to Mary Co-redemptrix and the supernatural effects of the Mother's providential role for humanity.[10] The theme of Mary Co-redemptrix is the major Mariological thread that runs throughout Sr. Lucia's extraordinary writings, second only to theme of the

Immaculate Heart of Mary (and certainly complementary to it). So instructive and inspiring are her theological meditations on Mary Co-redemptrix that we offer at considerable length her reflections, which so well integrate the title with the overall Fatima call to the contemporary world.

In her treatment on devotion to Mary's Immaculate Heart, Sr. Lucia acknowledges the unity of the Heart of Mary Co-redemptrix with the Heart of Christ from the Annunciation to Calvary:

> God began the work of our redemption in the Heart of Mary, given that it was through her "*fiat*" that the redemption began to come about: "And Mary said, *'Behold, I am the handmaid of the Lord; let it be done to me according to your word.'* (Lk. 1:38). *"And the Word became flesh and dwelt among us"* (Jn. 1:14). Thus, in the closest union possible between two human beings, Christ began, with Mary, the work of our salvation. The Christ's heart-beats are those of the heart of Mary, the prayer of Christ is the prayer of Mary, the joys of Christ are the joys of Mary; it was from Mary that Christ received the Body and Blood that are to be poured out and offered for the salvation of the world. Hence, Mary, made one with Christ, is the Co-redemptrix of the human race.

> With Christ in her womb, with Jesus Christ in her arms, with Christ at Nazareth and in his public life; with Christ she climbed the hill of Calvary, she suffered and agonized with Him, receiving into her Immaculate Heart the last sufferings of Christ, his last words, his last agony and the last drops of his Blood, in order to offer them to the Father.[11]

Sr. Lucia's commentary on the Presentation describes the Mother's knowledge of the eventual fulfillment of Simeon's prophecy and her expiatory offering "with Jesus" as Co-redemptrix of humanity:

> Mary knows that this prophecy is to be fulfilled in the person of her Son; she knows that He has been sent by God to carry out the work of our redemption. And far from wanting to save Him from such pain and suffering, she takes Him in her pure arms, brings Him to the temple with her virginal hands and places Him on the altar so that the priest may offer Him to the eternal Father as an expiatory victim and a sacrifice of praise.
>
> Here, Mary does not simply offer her Son, she offers herself with Christ, because Jesus had received his body and

> blood from her; thus she offers herself in and with Christ to God, Co-redemptrix, with Christ, of humanity.[12]

The powerful intercession by Mary, Mediatrix of all graces, in no way violates the scriptural revelation of 1 Timothy 2:5 of Christ, the One Mediator. Rather the Mother's subordinate participation in the mediation of Christ leads to the fulfillment of the redemptive mission of the One Mediator.[13] Sr. Lucia defends the Mother of God's intercessory power in virtue of her prior mission as Co-redemptrix:

> There is, thus, only one divine Mediator: Jesus Christ; but as supplicant intercessors we have Mary, the Saints, and each one of us, if we so wish. St. Paul himself, in various passages in his letters, asks people to pray both for him and for one another. *"To that end keep alert with all perseverance, making supplication for all the saints, and also for me, that utterance may be given in opening my mouth boldly to proclaim the mystery of the gospel, for which I am an ambassador in chains, that I may declare it boldly, as I ought to speak"* (Eph. 6:18-20).
>
> So if the Apostle tells us to pray for one another, we have much more reason to ask Mary to pray for us, because her

> prayer will be much more pleasing to the Lord in view of her dignity as Mother of God and her closer union with Christ, true God and true Man, by reason of her mission of Co-redemptrix with Christ as well as of her great sanctity.[14]

In the Fatima visionary's discussion of Our Lady's Assumption, she incorporates the coredemptive battle prophesied in Genesis 3:15 and the victorious "woman." The predestined Co-redemptrix of the human race is the first fruit of the Redemption, and hence could not remain in the "shadow of death":

> As soon as the first sin which brought condemnation on human beings had been committed, God, speaking to the Devil who had taken the form of a serpent and who had incited the first human beings to do evil, said to him: *"I will put enmity between you and the woman, and between your seed and her seed; he shall bruise your head, and you shall bruise his heel"* (Gen. 3:15).
>
> This woman, predestined by God to give Christ a human nature and to be, with Him, Co-redemptrix of the human race — *"I shall put enmity between you and the woman, and between your offspring and hers"* — this woman, He said, could not remain

> in the shadow of death, because she did not incur the sentence of punishment. Hence Mary is the first fruit of the Redemption wrought by Christ; and, through his merits, she was carried up to Heaven in body and soul, where she lives and reigns, in God, with her Son and his.[15]

The Fatima "call to holiness" voiced by the Carmelite visionary offers the Mother Co-redemptrix as our exemplary model in seeking holiness within the framework of our God-given vocations, just as the Immaculate Virgin "sanctified herself" as a wife and mother:

> Our Lady sanctified herself as a pure and immaculate virgin by corresponding to the graces which God granted to her in that state. She sanctified herself as a faithful and devoted wife by fulfilling all the duties of her state in life. She sanctified herself as a loving mother who dedicated herself to the Son whom God entrusted to her, fondling Him in her arms, bringing Him up and educating Him, and also helping Him and following Him in the performance of his mission. With Him she traveled the narrow way of life, the rugged road to Calvary; with Him she agonized, receiving in her heart the wounds of the nails, the piercing of the

> lance and the insults of the hostile crowd; finally, she sanctified herself as mother, mistress and guide of the Apostles, agreeing to remain on earth for as long as God wished, in order to accomplish the mission which He had entrusted to her as Co-redemptrix with Christ of all human beings.[16]

Finally, Sr. Lucia evokes the calling of all Christians to become co-redeemers in the work of salvation. What is our contribution to Redemption, she asks, and how can it be mysteriously efficacious for others? She answers with exceptional humility, and yet with penetrating insight into Redemption, the unity of the Two Hearts, and our Eucharistic Jesus, given to us by the Virgin Mother Co-redemptrix:

> And our own contribution? It is our humble prayer, our poor little acts of self-denial which we must unite with the prayer and sacrifice of Jesus Christ and of the Immaculate Heart of Mary in reparation, and for the salvation of our poor brothers and sisters who have wandered away from the one true path that leads to Life.
>
> At this point, I ask myself: Why is it that, since the merits and prayer of Jesus Christ are sufficient to make reparation for

and to save the world, the Message invokes the merits of the Immaculate Heart of Mary and calls on us, too, to pray, to make sacrifices, to offer reparation?

I have to say that I do not know! Nor do I know what explanation the theologians of the Church would give me if I were to ask them. But I have meditated on, and thought about this question. I open the Gospel and I see that from the very beginning Jesus Christ united to his redemptive work the Immaculate Heart of Her whom He chose to be his Mother.

The work of our redemption began at the moment when the Word descended from Heaven in order to assume a human body in the womb of Mary. From that moment, and for the next nine months, the blood of Christ was the blood of Mary, taken from her Immaculate Heart; the Heart of Christ was beating in unison with the Heart of Mary.

And we can think that the aspirations of the Heart of Mary were completely identified with the aspirations of the Heart of Christ. Mary's ideal had become the same as that of Christ Himself, and the love in the Heart of Mary was the love in the Heart of Christ for the Father and for all human beings; to begin with, the entire work of redemption passed through the Immaculate Heart of Mary, through the bond of her close intimate union with the divine Word.

Since the Father entrusted his Son to Mary, enclosing Him for nine months within her chaste virginal womb — and *"All this took place to fulfil what the Lord had spoken by the prophet: 'Behold, a virgin shall conceive and bear a son, and his name shall be called Emmanuel' (which means, God with us)."* (Mt. 1, 22-23; Is. 7:14). — and since Mary of her own free will opened herself entirely to whatever God willed to accomplish in her — *"Behold, I am the handmaid of the Lord; let it be done to me according to your word."* (Lk. 1:38) is what she said to the angel — in view of all this and by God's disposition, Mary became, with Christ, the Co-redemptrix of the human race.

It is the body received from Mary that, in Christ, becomes a victim offered up for the salvation of mankind; it is the blood received from Mary that circulates in Christ's veins and which pours out from his divine Heart; it is this same body and this same blood, received from Mary, that are given to us, under the appearances of bread and wine, as our daily food, to strengthen within us the life of grace, and so continue in us, members of the Mystical Body of Christ, his redemptive work for the salvation of each and all to the extent to which each one clings to Christ and co-operates with Christ.

Thus, having led us to offer to the Most Holy Trinity the merits of Jesus Christ and those of the Immaculate Heart of Mary, who is the Mother of Christ and of his Mystical Body, the Message then goes on to ask us to contribute also the prayers and sacrifices of all of us who are members of that one same Body of Christ received from Mary, made divine in the Word, offered on the Cross, present in the Eucharist, constantly growing in the members of the Church.

Since she is the Mother of Christ and of his Mystical body, the Immaculate Heart of Mary is in some sense the Heart of the Church: and it is here in the heart of the Church that she, always united with Christ, watches over the members of the Church, granting them her maternal protection. Better than anyone, Mary fulfils Christ's injunction: *"Hitherto you have asked nothing in my name; ask, and you will receive, that your joy may be full."* (Jn. 16:24). It is in the name of Christ, her Son, that Mary intercedes for us with the Father. And it is in the name of Christ, present in the Eucharist and united with us in Holy Communion, that we unite our humble prayers with those of Mary so that She can address them to the Father in Jesus Christ, her Son.

Hence it is that over and over again we beseech Her: *"Holy Mary, Mother of God, pray for us, sinners, now and at the hour of our death. Amen."*

Ave Maria![17]

Notes

[1] July 13, 1917 Fatima apparition, cf. A. Martins, S.J., *Novos Documentos de Fátima*, Porto, 1984, translated into English as *Documents on Fatima and the Memoirs of Sister Lucia*, Fatima Family Apostolate, 1992, p. 401.

[2] Technically an apparition message from the "Angel of Peace" (not directly from Our Lady, but at the same time part of the Fatima message), Second 1916 Fatima apparition, cf. *Documents on Fatima and the Memoirs*, p. 396.

[3] May 13, 1917 Fatima apparition, cf. *Documents on Fatima and the Memoirs*, p. 399.

[4] *Ibid.*

[5] John Paul II, Beatification of Jacinta and Francisco, May 13, 2000, *L'Osservatore Romano*, May 17, 2000.

[6] For reference, the first two parts of the July 13 message are given here, followed by the "Third Part." Reference to particular sufferings by the Holy Father are contained in the July 13 message and also in the "Third Part" of the secret of Fatima, released by John Paul II on May 13, 2000, and published in the June 28, 2000, *L'Osservatore Romano*, English edition, followed by the Vatican commentary on the Third Part which cited Sr. Lucia's identification of the "bishop in white" as specifically referring to John Paul II:

"Some moments after we arrived at Cova da Iria, near the holm oak amongst a big crowd of people, when we were praying the Rosary, we saw the radiance of light and afterwards our Lady over the holm oak.

'What do you want of me?' I asked.

'I want you to come here on the thirteenth day of the coming month, and to continue to say the Rosary every day in honor of our Lady of the Rosary to obtain the peace of the world and the end of the war. For she alone will be able to help.'

'I wish to ask you to tell us who you are and to perform a miracle so that everyone will believe that you appeared to us!'

'Continue to come here every month. In October I will tell you who I am and what I wish, and I will perform a miracle that everyone will see in order to make them believe.'

Here I made some requests that I don't remember exactly. What I remember is that our Lady said it was necessary to say the Rosary to obtain graces during the year. And she went on, 'Sacrifice yourselves for sinners and say many times, especially when you make some sacrifice: "Jesus it is for Your love, for the conversion of sinners and in reparation for the sins committed against the Immaculate Heart of Mary."'

When the Lady spoke these last words she opened her hands as she had in the two months before. The radiance seemed to penetrate the ground and we saw something like a sea of fire. Plunged in this fire were the demons and the souls, as if they were red hot coals, transparent and black or bronze colored, with human forms, which floated about in the conflagration, borne by the flames which issued from it with clouds of smoke falling on all sides as sparks fell in great conflagrations without weight or equilibrium, among shrieks and groans of sorrow and despair that horrify and cause people to shudder with fear. It must have been when I saw this sight that I cried out, 'Alas!' which people say they heard.

The devils were distinguished by horrible and loathsome forms of animals, frightful and unknown, but transparent like black coals that have turned red hot. Frightened, and as if we were appealing for help, we raised our eyes to our Lady who said with tenderness and sadness:

'You saw hell, where the souls of poor sinners go. To save them God wishes to establish in the world the devotion to my Immaculate Heart. If they do what I will tell you, many souls will be saved, and there will be peace. The war is going to end. But if they do not stop offending God, another even worse war will begin in the reign of Pius XI.

When you see a night illuminated by an unknown light, know that it is the great sign that God gives you that He is going to punish the world for its crimes by means of war, hunger and persecutions of the Church and of the Holy Father.

To prevent this I will come to ask for the consecration of Russia to my Immaculate Heart and the Communion of reparation on the first Saturdays. If they listen to my requests, Russia will be converted and there will be peace. If not, she will scatter her errors throughout the world, provoking wars and persecutions of the Church. The good will be martyred, the Holy Father will have much to suffer, and various nations will be annihilated. In the end my Immaculate Heart will triumph. The Holy Father will consecrate Russia to me, and it will be converted and a certain period of peace will be granted to the world. In Portugal the dogma of Faith will always be kept. Tell this to no one. Francisco, yes, you may tell him. When you say the Rosary, say after each mystery, "O my Jesus, pardon us and deliver us from the fire of hell. Draw all souls to heaven, especially those in most need."'

After a short period of silence, I asked, 'Do you want nothing more of me?'

'No, today I want nothing more of you.'

And as usual, she began to arise towards the east and disappeared in the immense distance of the firmament."

The Third Part of the secret released by John Paul II in 2000 reads as follows:

"J.M.J. The third part of the secret revealed at the Cova da Iria-Fatima, on 13 July 1917.

I write in obedience to you, my God, who command me to do so through his Excellency the Bishop of Leiria and through your Most Holy Mother and mine.

After the two parts which I have already explained, at the left of Our Lady and a little above, we saw an Angel with a flaming sword in his left hand; flashing, it gave out flames that looked as though they would set the world on fire; but they died out in contact with the splendour that Our Lady radiated towards him from her right hand: pointing to the earth with his right hand, the Angel cried out in a loud voice: '*Penance, Penance, Penance!*' And we saw in an immense light that is God, something similar to how people appear in a mirror when they pass in front of it, a Bishop dressed in White; we had the impression that it was the Holy Father. Other Bishops, Priests, men and women Religious going up a steep mountain, at the top of which there was a big Cross of rough-hewn trunks as of a cork-tree with the bark; before reaching there the Holy Father passed through a big city half in ruins and half trembling with halting step, afflicted with pain and sorrow, he prayed for the souls of the corpses he met on his way; having reached the top of the mountain, on his knees at the foot of the big Cross he was killed by a group of soldiers who fired bullets and arrows at him, and in the same way there died one after another the other Bishops, Priests, men and women Religious, and various lay people of different ranks and positions. Beneath the two arms of the Cross there were two Angels each with a crystal aspersorium in his hand, in which they gathered up the blood of the Martyrs and with it sprinkled the souls that were making their way to God.

Tuy-3-1-1944."

[7] July 13, 1917 Fatima apparition, cf. *Documents on Fatima and the Memoirs*, p. 401.

[8] October 13, 1917 Fatima apparition, cf. *Documents on Fatima and the Memoirs*, p. 405.

[9] July 13, 1917 Fatima apparition, cf. *Documents on Fatima and the Memoirs*, p. 402.

[10] Sr. Lucia, *"Calls" From the Message of Fatima*, Ravengate Press, 2002, originally published in Portuguese under the title *Apelos da Messagem de Fatima*.

[11] Sr. Lucia, *"Calls" From the Message of Fatima*, p. 137.

[12] *Ibid.*, p. 279.

[13] Cf. *Lumen Gentium*, 61, 62.

[14] Sr. Lucia, *"Calls" From the Message of Fatima*, p. 266.

[15] *Ibid.*, p. 295.

[16] *Ibid.*, p. 195.

[17] *Ibid.*, pp. 114-116.

Conclusion

Mary Co-redemptrix is our heritage. The story of Mary "with Jesus" is deeply imbedded in the Church's two thousand year Memory and Life which we call "Tradition." The Immaculate Co-redemptrix is hailed in our Scriptures. It is a truth we should glory in, a Christian mystery we should contemplate in imitation of the angels.

She is a Mother whom we should thank with every fiber of our heart in eternal gratitude for an immaculate suffering beyond all human imagination.

The doctrine of Mary Co-redemptrix will one day be crowned as a dogma. It is not a matter of "if," but "when." The doctrinal development of the Mother Suffering, which is vivified by the Holy Spirit can never go backward, but only forward.

"In God's good time." Sometimes this phrase is used to remind us of the sovereignty of God, Author of time and director of Providence. At other times, it can be used as a form of human excuse for the lack of adequate co-operation by man with the Providence of God. Such lack always results in a loss of grace for humanity.

The Dogma of the Co-redemptrix will be. May its dogmatic proclamation come soon, as humanity's "yes" to the Mother's saving role for us. May it come soon to "release" the Immaculate Mother within that mysterious order of Providence and free will, so that she may exercise fully her necessary intercession for peace and grace in today's troubled world.

When she is dogmatically crowned, I believe two prophetic hymns to Mary Co-redemptrix, one from each Testament of God's inspired word, will be profoundly fulfilled:

> "*I exalt my God;*
> *and my spirit rejoices in the King of heaven,*
> *A bright light shall shine*
> *over all the regions of the earth;*
> *And the name of her who is Elect shall endure*
> *through the generations to come.*" (Tobit 13:7,11).
>
> "*My soul magnifies the Lord,*
> *and my spirit rejoices in God my Savior,*
> *for he has regarded the humility of his handmaid.*
> *For behold, from this day, all generations*
> *will call me blessed*" (Lk. 1:46-48).